FEB - - 2005

SCOTTSDALE BRANCH
4101 WEST 79th STREET
CHICAGO, ILLINOIS 60652

TAOISM
WORLD RELIGIONS

by
Paula R. Hartz

Facts On File, Inc.

TAOISM, Updated Edition

World Religions

Facts On File, Inc.
132 West 31st Street
New York NY 10001

Library of Congress Cataloging-in-Publication Data

Hartz, Paula.
    Taoism / by Paula R. Hartz.—Updated ed.
        p. cm.—(World religions)
    Includes bibliographical references and index.
        ISBN 0-8160-5724-9
        1. Taoism I. Title. II. Series
BL1920.H37 2004
299.5'14—dc22   2004043224

Facts On File books are available at special discounts when purchased in bulk quantities for businesses, associations, institutions, or sales promotions. Please call our Special Sales Department in New York at 212/967-8800 or 800/322-8755.

You can find Facts On File on the World Wide Web at http://www.factsonfile.com

Developed by Brown Publishing Network, Inc.

Photo Research by Susan Van Etten

Photo credits:

Cover: The twenty-eight constellations personified, 1454. China, Ming dynasty, reign of Xuande. © Réunion des Musées Nationaux/Art Resource, New York; Title page: The Three Pure Ones, the highest deities of Taoism. From left to right: the Primordial Being, the Jade Emperor, Laozi. Table of Contents page: Family members pay tribute to their ancestors as part of the New Year celebration. Marburg/Art Resource, NY. Pages *6-7* Bohemian Nomad Picturemakers/CORBIS; *10* P. Stephenson/Envision; *14* The Nelson-Atkins Museum of Art, Kansas City, MO (Gift of Bronson Trevor in honor of his father, John Trevor) 76-10/12.; *16-17* Detail from 16.114. © Smithsonian Institution, courtesy of the Freer Gallery of Art; *21* Asian Art Museum of San Francisco, The Avery Brundage Collection; *23* Marburg/Art Resource, NY; *32* Asian Art & Archaeology/Art Resource, NY; *34-35* ©.Susan Van Etten; *38* Asian Art Museum of San Francisco, The Avery Brundage Collection; *44* Marburg/Art Resource, NY; *50* 61.34 © Smithsonian Institution, courtesy of the Freer Gallery of Art; *56-57* © Pablo San Juan/CORBIS; *62* Philadelphia Museum of Art. Given by Miss Anne Rowland; *65* © Peter Turnley/CORBIS; *70* The Nelson-Atkins Museum of Art, Kansas City, MO (Nelson Fund) 62-25; *72* Asian Art & Archaeology/Art Resource, NY; *74-75* Info Div. of CCNAA, Office in Boston; *80* Asian Art & Archaeology/Art Resource, NY; *81 & 83* Info Div. of CCNAA, Office in Boston; *84 & 90* AP/Wide World; *94-95* ©AFP/CORBIS; *100* Asian Art Museum of San Francisco, The Avery Brundage Collection; *102* Founders Society Purchase, General Membership and Donations Fund. © The Detroit Institute of Arts 1991; *104* Asian Art Museum of San Francisco, The Avery Brundage Collection; *105* Asian Art Museum of San Francisco, The Avery Brundage Collection. Gift of the Asian Art Foundation of San Francisco; *107* Asian Art Museum of San Franciscom, The Avery Brundage Collection; *110-111* © James Marshall/CORBIS; *113* Bettmann/CORBIS; China Program; *115* Pablo San Juan/CORBIS; *116* © Mike McQueen/CORBIS; *118* Royalty-Free/CORBIS.

Printed in the United States of America

VB PKG 10 9 8 7 6 5 4 3 2 1

This book is printed on acid-free paper.

TABLE OF CONTENTS

	Preface	4
CHAPTER 1	Introduction: The Modern Taoist World	6
CHAPTER 2	The Origins and Early History of Taoism	16
CHAPTER 3	The Growth and Spread of Religious Taoism	34
CHAPTER 4	The Scriptures and Beliefs of Taoism	56
CHAPTER 5	Ritual and Meditation	74
CHAPTER 6	The Tao of the Arts	94
CHAPTER 7	Taoism Yesterday, Today, and Tomorrow	110
	Chapter Notes	122
	Glossary	123
	For Further Reading	125
	Index	126

Preface

We live in what is sometimes described as a "secular age," meaning, in effect, that religion is not an especially important issue for most people. But there is much evidence to the contrary. In many societies, including the United States, religion and religious values shape the lives of millions of individuals and play a key role in politics and culture as well.

The World Religions series, of which this book is a part, is designed to appeal to both students and general readers. The books offer clear, accessible overviews of the major religious traditions and institutions of our time. Each volume in the series describes where a particular religion is practiced, its origins and history, its central beliefs and important rituals, and its contributions to world civilization. Carefully chosen photographs complement the text, and a glossary and bibliography are included to help readers gain a more complete understanding of the subject at hand.

Religious institutions and spirituality have always played a central role in world history. These books will help clarify what religion is all about and reveal both the similarities and differences in the great spiritual traditions practiced around the world today.

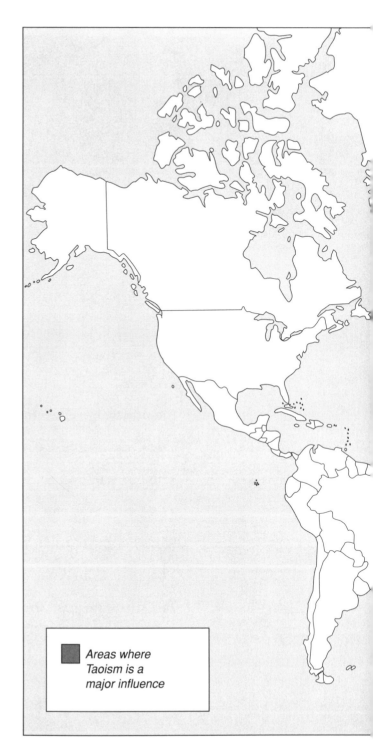

Areas where Taoism is a major influence

CHAPTER 1

Introduction: The Modern Taoist World

*T*aoism (pronounced DOW-ism) is one of the two great philosophical and religious traditions that originated in China. The other religion native to China is Confucianism. Both Taoism and Confucianism began at about the same time, around the sixth century B.C.E. (before the common era), or between 500 and 400 B.C. China's third great tradition, Buddhism, came to China from India around the second century of the common era. Together, these three faiths have shaped Chinese life and thought for nearly twenty-five hundred years.

The number of people worldwide who consider themselves Taoists is relatively small—around thirty-one million—compared to about three hundred million Buddhists, for example. In the West, Taoism's influence has been comparatively slight. However, Taoist thought and philosophy can be found in almost every aspect of Chinese life, both in Asia and around the world.

Wherever the Chinese people have gone, they have taken Taoism with them. Thus, elements of Taoism appear in many of the countries that came under Chinese influence over the centuries—countries such as Korea, Vietnam, and Japan—and in the

Chinese sections of Western cities in Europe, Canada, and the United States. Taoism has also had a strong influence on Chinese literature and on the technique and subject matter of Chinese art.

About three million of the world's Taoists live on the island of Taiwan, off the coast of China. When the Chinese mainland fell to communism in 1949, religion was banned. The celestial master of Taoism, the head of the faith, fled to Taiwan and continues to live there to this day. The People's Republic of China is officially atheist, so it is hard to know how many of its people are Taoists; but it is estimated that the number is large and growing. Since the Chinese government now allows people to practice religion again, many Taoist temples have been restored and Taoism is on the rise.

What Is Taoism?

In Chinese, the word *tao* means "the way." Simply put, the way is understood to mean the way of nature. Taoists see the cycles of nature and the constant change in the natural world as earthly signs of a great and universal force. They call this unseen force Tao.

For some, Tao is the Ultimate Reality, a presence that existed before the universe was formed and which continues to guide the world and everything in it. Tao is sometimes identified as the Mother, or the source of all things. However, that source is not a god or a supreme being, for unlike Christianity, Islam, and Judaism, Taoism is not monotheistic. Its followers do not worship one god; practitioners focus instead on coming into harmony with Tao.

Unlike many other world religions, Taoism has no one founder. It has no central figure like Christ, Buddha, Mohammed, or Confucius. Instead, it has a number of masters. The great Taoist masters were men who taught or wrote about Tao or who commented on the writings of others. Taoists look to the works of those masters to help them find "the way." This may not be easy, for according to the Taoist masters, Tao can be learned, but it cannot be taught.

Look, and it can't be seen.
Listen, and it can't be heard.

Reach, and it can't be grasped. . . .
You can't know it, but you can be it,
at ease in your own life.

Taoists say that the Tao that can be expressed in words is not the real or "eternal" Tao. Masters and writers can help to point the way, but each person must find his or her own Tao.

Taoism reaches not only into the intellectual and spiritual lives of its followers but also into their physical life. Taoists see the physical body as a kind of microcosm, or miniature model, of the universe. They ask: How can a person be in harmony with the universe if his or her body is not in harmony with itself? Thus, to a Taoist, the way in which someone treats his or her body is as important as what that person thinks, believes, or does in relation to others.

■ *Many Chinese families rely on the herbal medicines that were developed by Taoist alchemists and herbalists in the early centuries of the common era.*

Taoists believe that a healthy body is a necessary first step to achieving a lofty spiritual state. Thus, Taoism has long been associated with certain medicinal and nutritional practices. Many of the ideas and practices that Westerners think of as Chinese or Asian are, in fact, Taoist. For example, acupressure and acupuncture, Eastern medical arts that in the past few years have been the subject of study in Western medicine, were developed by Taoist masters and have been in use for centuries.

Taoist masters have recorded the medicinal uses of thousands of plants—trees, herbs, flowers, fruits, and fungi—and have studied nutrition. The masters recommend a prudent, balanced diet to maintain health and to promote longevity. Taoist recommendations on diet are quite different, however, from the dietary laws of religions such as Judaism and Hinduism, which ask their followers to abstain from certain foods as part of their religious observance. Taoists forbid nothing, recommending only that substances harmful to the body be avoided and that everything else be eaten and drunk in a balanced, sensible, healthful way. To the Taoist, for example, broccoli is a good food, but a diet that consists only of broccoli is not good because it is not balanced, and balance is the Taoist way.

In addition to a healthful diet, exercise is an integral part of Taoist practice. According to legend, an early Taoist master named Zhang San Feng watched the movements of birds and animals and sought to copy them as a way of getting closer to the natural state. He became known as the founder of *taijiquan (t'ai chi ch'uan)*, the ancient form of Chinese exercise. Taiji exercises are used to control *qi (ch'i)*, or "breath," an essential element of human existence, which for Taoists is the center of spiritual, emotional, and physical health. The stretching, bending, and flexing exercises embody the natural qi of the animals, and dispel the physical tensions that keep people from finding inner peace and being in touch with Tao.

Meditation is often associated with Buddhism and other faiths from India; but long before Buddhism came to China, Taoists were using a form of meditation to help them come into harmony with the ultimate reality of the universe. The concept of *wuwei*, or "non-doing," is central to Taoist meditation. It is the practice of quietism—of letting go all worldly thought and action so that Tao may enter. The phrase *wei wuwei* literally means "to do without doing," or "to act without action," but this literal translation does not express the complete meaning. The concept of wuwei more closely suggests a way of existing without conscious effort, as nature does.

Taoists believe that time spent in meditation prolongs life. In Taoist belief, longevity is important, because the longer one lives, the greater one's chances are of achieving perfect harmony with Tao. The perfect person might hope to become immortal and rise to heaven—not just in spirit, but physically as well. A number of legendary and historical people are believed to have reached this immortal state called *xian*. Worshipers ask these immortals of Taoism to help them, much as some Christians ask saints for help.

The immortals of Taoism include emperors, Taoist masters, heroes of battle, and ordinary people who have attained this exalted condition through suffering, heroic deeds, or service to others.

Taoists continue to strive toward xian, oneness with the universe, perfecting their bodies as well as their minds.

Over the centuries, the threads of Confucianism, Buddhism, and Taoism have become intertwined, each absorbing aspects of the others. As the Chinese say, "The three teachings flow into one." This blending of traditions is consistent with the Asian approach to religion, which allows for believing in more than one truth. Thus, many people who consider themselves Chinese Buddhists or Confucianists, as well as many agnostics—people who claim that no one can know whether a god exists but who do not deny the possibility of that existence—also practice aspects of Taoism. Such practice is possible because the traditions do not conflict. Rather, they complement one another.

■ A Note on Chinese Spellings

Chinese names and words in this book are written in Pinyin, a system of writing Chinese by using the roman alphabet. This system was adopted by the People's Republic of China in 1979. Its developers hoped to make Chinese easier to read by providing standard spellings, thus encouraging non-Chinese to learn the language by making it easier to read than older alphabetical systems.

For the most part, words in Pinyin are pronounced the way they are spelled. There are a few exceptions, however:

Consonants	Vowels
*c is pronounced like **ts***	*e before ng is pronounced like **u** in **sung***
*q is pronounced like **ch** in **chip***	
*x is pronounced like **sh** in **show***	*o is pronounced like **aw** in **jaw***
*zh is pronounced like **j** in **jot***	*ou is pronounced like **o** in **go***

*In many sources, Chinese words appear in alphabet systems used before Pinyin was adopted, most of which are still used in Taiwan today. In the West, many of those Chinese words are more familiar in the older form. One such word is **Taoism,** which has always been pronounced DOWism. In Pinyin, **Taoism** is written as **Daoism.** Most dictionaries, encyclopedias, and library catalogues use the **Taoism** spelling, however, and that is the spelling used in this book.*

The Variety of Taoism

Taoists have never made an attempt to spread their religion. Travelers and wanderers, but never missionaries, they do not visit other countries to win converts. Taoist masters prefer to let students come to them and to counsel them one on one. Many early masters did gather followers, however, and a number of sects resulted. Taoists tend to see the differing interpretations of their beliefs as part of the infinite variety of the universe rather than as right or wrong. Over the centuries, Taoism has had many masters and many interpretations.

Like Buddhism, Taoism has different levels. In its purest form, it can be the basis for a life of contemplation and prayer. However, it also addresses the concerns of ordinary people, offering calm and inner peace, a way to health and long life, and forgiveness of sin through rituals and good works.

In all, Taoists seek balance and harmony in their lives. Their ideas are often associated with the concept of yin and yang, the interaction between opposite forces in nature. In Chinese thought, yin, "the shady side of the hill," cannot exist without yang, "the sunny side." To have one, it is necessary to have the other. Yin is passive; yang is active. Yin is cool yang is warm. Yin is night; yang is day. Yin is female; yang is male. Taoism celebrates yin, the femaleness of the universe, in which quiet and "letting be" are more fruitful than strife and direct action.

Taoism and the Three Traditions

Taoism shares with Confucianism and Buddhism many of the attributes that make them different from Western religions. Like Buddhists and Confucianists, Taoists do not attend regularly scheduled worship services or make statements of faith. There is no specific creed to which they must subscribe. While there are many traditional observances and rituals, there are none in which a follower must participate in order to be a Taoist.

Unlike followers of Christianity or Islam or Judaism, Taoists, Buddhists, and Confucianists do not believe in a supreme being or in the immortality of the soul. Believers in Western traditions are concerned with the love of people for God, but religion in China has long concerned itself with practical moral behavior

■ *On this scroll, the main figures of China's three religious traditions appear together, signifying the harmony among them. Buddha is on the left, Confucius in the center, and Taoism's Laozi on the right.*

and self-improvement. Like the other "great truths," Taoism provides guidance for living a moral life and attempts to explain the place of human beings in the natural universe. Some of Taoism's ancient practices for health and serenity attract followers of their own.

Thus, Taoism accommodates many points of view and practices. Taoist monks and nuns may retreat from the world and live in monasteries, trying to achieve spiritual perfection and become one with Tao. Taoist priests may live and work among the people, performing ancient rituals for health, prosperity, and redemption from sin. Some individuals may follow a particular Taoist practice such as taijiquan or meditation, or they may pursue an interest in Chinese medicine. Others may follow the religious rituals of Taoism in their homes, lighting incense to the spirits of their ancestors and the Taoist gods. All of these people consider themselves Taoists. They are all part of the living religion, examples of its vitality and strength.

CHAPTER 2

The Origins and Early History of Taoism

Scholars believe that Taoism began as a way of thinking around the sixth century B.C.E. But the roots of Taoist thought are much older than that. They are as old as the oldest legends and beliefs of the Chinese people. For many Taoist believers, Taoism can be traced to the great and wise ruler Huang Di, also known as the Yellow Emperor.

Huang Di was one of several legendary emperors who lived before recorded history. Stories about him appear in many ancient sources. He is said to have ruled from 2696 to 2598 B.C.E., almost one hundred years.

According to legend, in the nineteenth year of his reign, Huang Di traveled into the mountains to consult a very old and wise hermit about the secret of life. At first, the recluse would not answer Huang Di's questions. But at last Huang Di succeeded in his quest, and he came away with great knowledge—knowledge that he applied to many areas of life and government. Thus, Huang Di is revered not only for having been a wise and just emperor but also for having been the first to diagnose and cure many diseases, to use magic to tame wild animals, and to use military strategy effectively.

But the legend continues. The hermit explained to Huang Di that he had lived to be twelve hundred years old by dwelling in Tao, or in harmony with the universe. Huang Di adopted the hermit's principles, and at the end of his glorious ninety-nine-year reign, he rode off to heaven on the back of a dragon and thus became immortal.

This legend expresses a longing that has existed since before recorded time. Even then, people were searching for the right way to live so that they, too, might enjoy endless life. One "way" came to be called Taoism.

The Golden Age of Philosophy

Recorded Chinese history begins more than fifteen hundred years before the common era. The first ruling dynasty (family) of record was the Shang dynasty, which began around 1700 B.C.E. The records describe cities, social classes, a calendar, and an organized government. In 1027 B.C.E., after approximately seven hundred years of Shang rule, the Zhou (Chou) dynasty came into power. The Zhou rulers remained in charge for almost eight hundred years.

The Zhou dynasty began in a dynamic way. During its reign, written laws were developed, money came into use, and farming took a giant step forward with the invention of an iron plow. But after several hundred years, widespread political corruption and disorder began to take over. The people began to long for the simpler, happier life of ancient times. They wanted direction, and to find it, they turned to philosophers and sages—the great thinkers and writers of the age. This period became known as the Golden Age of Philosophy. It produced several men whose works have endured over the centuries and on whose thoughts and teachings the great religious traditions of China are based.

Confucius

One of the great thinkers of the Golden Age was Confucius, who was born around 551 B.C.E. Confucius believed that the cure for the problems of society was moral, ethical behavior. He traveled from court to court, trying to convince rulers to govern according to his plan.

Confucius rejected all that was violent, disorderly, strange, or supernatural. His teachings recommended respect for the gods and concentration on relationships between people. He set rules for relationships: the equal relationship of friend to friend, and the hierarchical relationship between parent and child, ruler and subject, husband and wife, and older and younger siblings. His rules stressed loyalty, decency, trustworthiness, and propriety.

The Confucian ideal society was one in which the emperor cared for his subjects as a loving father would and his subjects obeyed as loving children; one in which younger would obey older and wiser and all would live in harmony in a family.

Confucius taught principles of moral behavior. He felt that a person who lived by his rules would develop the habit of ethical behavior. Eventually this behavior would become deeply ingrained in one's personality. The person who followed his principles would thus achieve virtue.

Confucius advised people to respect the good example of others, to behave properly toward all, and to be prudent and follow the middle course. "The cautious seldom make mistakes," he said. He also stressed the importance of studying the *Five Classics*, the collection of books that summarized the wisdom and thought of China. He suggested that emperors hire scholars to study the works of the great thinkers in Chinese history. The scholars would then be able to convey their accumulated wisdom to the emperors and their courts. In this way, all that was good, fitting, and proper in Chinese tradition would become integrated with current society.

The followers of Confucius gathered all of his sayings and parables, simple stories that illustrate a moral, in a work known as the *Analects*. Confucianism, as the tradition that came from the teachings of Confucius was called, stressed rules of conduct and etiquette. It promoted ritual as the way to harmony between people and God; it promoted rules of behavior to create harmony between individuals and within society at large.

Confucianism appealed to the practical minds and common sense of the Chinese people. In China's bustling, crowded cities and palaces, it provided a framework within which the people could structure their lives and conduct business and government.

Confucianism was a yardstick by which to measure one's own conduct and the conduct of others, a standard for choosing officials and business associates. In times of war and government corruption, it was a clear path to follow. It won many adherents.

Not everyone agreed with the ideas of Confucius, however. Some people felt that Confucianism focused too much on society and government and not enough on the relationship of people to the natural world. Its emphasis on rules of conduct and the ethical treatment of others in society did not satisfy an inner hunger of the spirit. Nor was it in keeping with many of the existing beliefs of those who lived close to the earth.

With their ancient farming culture, many Chinese felt closer to the forces of nature than to the problems of government. Popular religious practice reflected this connection. People honored their ancestors, local gods, the gods of the heavens, and the gods of the earth. They believed that the spirits of great leaders continued to exist and that their spiritual powers could be called upon. Close observation of nature had convinced the people that there was a pattern in the universe and an unseen, perhaps unknowable, force behind it.

Legends of mountain men, or hermits, in China came from a time before written history. The tales told of people who had withdrawn from society, seeking to understand the connection between human life and the natural world. The tradition continued for thousands of years. The mountain men of Confucius' time, like mystics of all faiths, believed that knowledge and understanding of the unseen came through personal experience, not through the senses or through study. These mountain men rejected the Confucian way to a good and moral life. They felt that by withdrawing to a serene place and becoming one with nature, they could find "the Way."

Laozi

Like the Yellow Emperor centuries before him, the man on whose teachings Taoism is based is semi-legendary. No one is really sure whether or not he existed. It has been suggested that he was not one person but a composite of many wise men of his time. Still, the earliest history of China, written around the second

century B.C.E., includes a biographical sketch of this man. It says that his name was Li Ehr and that he was Confucius' contemporary, although slightly older than Confucius.

Little is known about his life. According to tradition, he worked as the archivist in the royal palace in Luoyang, the capital of the Zhou dynasty. There he became known as Laozi (Lao Tzu), which is not a name, but a title meaning "The Old One" or "The Master." Sometimes he was called Lao Dan, which means "Old Big Ear."

According to tradition, Laozi grew in wisdom during his lifetime and many people consulted him on the questions of religion and politics. A source written some two hundred years after Laozi's lifetime reveals the legendary details of a meeting between Laozi and Confucius in Luoyang. Laozi was known for his virtue and his wise teachings, but he was apparently crusty and

■ *For Taoists, mountains are especially spiritual places. In this jade carving, Taoist travelers wend their way along a mountain trail toward a solitary Taoist and the temple at the top.*

sharp-tongued. He was impatient with Confucius' practical ways and challenged the belief that knowledge and learning, not to mention a code of behavior, would help people improve. People, he suggested, were born good and needed nothing to keep them that way except to be left alone. Certainly there was no point, he felt, in studying the works of past masters. "All the men of which you speak have long since mouldered away to their bones," Laozi snapped to Confucius. "Give up your proud airs, your many wishes, mannerisms, and extravagant claims. They won't do you any good! That's all I have to tell you."

After the meeting, Confucius remarked, "I know that birds can fly and fish can swim and beasts can run. Snares can be set for things that run, nets for those that swim, and arrows for whatever flies. But dragons! I shall never know how they ride wind and cloud up into the sky. Today I saw Laozi. What a dragon!"

Laozi worked in the royal archives of the Zhou court until he was over ninety years old. By that time, the dynasty was in its decline. Tired of government work, he decided to leave the province. As he traveled through a mountain pass, riding on a water buffalo, he was recognized by a border guard. The guard was distressed to think that the wisdom of this great sage would be lost to the kingdom forever. He asked Laozi to record his wise thoughts before leaving the province.

According to the story, Laozi sat down then and there and wrote out a little manuscript, only five thousand Chinese characters long. He gave it to the guard; then he left the province and was not heard from again. The manuscript he left behind is known as the *Laozi*, or, more commonly, the *Tao Te Ching (Daodejing)*, "The Book of the Way and Its Power."

The *Tao Te Ching*

The *Tao Te Ching* is a collection of eighty-one short poems, which are called chapters. Scholars today feel that the *Tao Te Ching* is not the work of one person but rather a collection of the works of many people, gathered over a period of time, probably during the fourth century B.C.E., about two hundred years after Laozi's lifetime. Still, the *Tao Te Ching*, with its philosophical beliefs, is traditionally attributed to Laozi.

■ *Tradition holds that after many years of service as a royal librarian, Laozi rode into the mountains on a water buffalo and became immortal. On his way, he stopped to write the **Tao Te Ching,** the foundation of Taoist scripture.*

Whether the *Tao Te Ching* is the work of one or of many, certainly its writer or writers were drawing on a tradition already thousands of years old when the book was created. The poems are tightly written in a very few words, and people have discussed and debated their meanings for centuries, much as they do the meaning of the writings in the Judeo-Christian Bible.

Many of the poems are addressed to a ruler and give advice on how to govern. The advice is surprising in some ways. For example, instead of saying, "Be strong; rule with a firm hand," Laozi counsels, "Be weak; let things alone." He counsels humility and inaction, saying that rulers who interfere in the lives of the people are asking for trouble.

Sometimes the statements in the book are expressed in paradoxes—statements that seem to contradict themselves. For example:

> *True mastery can be gained*
> *by letting things go their own way.*
> *It can't be gained by interfering.*

And later,

> *Seeing into darkness is clarity.*
> *Knowing how to yield is strength.*

At first glance, these statements may indeed seem contradictory. How can a ruler rule without ruling? Yet Laozi's ideas are consistent. What is low cannot fall, and what bends does not break. He suggests handling small problems before they become big ones; he points out that by rushing in, people make mistakes that are hard to undo. "The Tao," Laozi says, "is always at ease. It overcomes without competing, answers without speaking a word, arrives without being summoned, accomplishes without a plan."

According to Laozi, Tao teaches the unimportance of importance. Water takes the low, or unimportant, path as it seeps into the ground. Unnoticed, it is the nourishing force that sustains plants, people, and animals. The lower it sinks, the more truly important it is. Laozi says:

> *The supreme good is like water,*
> *Which nourishes all things without trying to.*
> *It is content to take the low places that people disdain.*
> *Thus it is like the Tao.*

Like water, Tao gives birth to and nourishes everything but makes no claim to importance. Like water, the wise person will work without calling attention to himself or herself, will do what is right and fair, and will become attuned to the nature of things. That person will understand Tao. People must learn to seek Tao, which is unimportant in the sense that it is not noticeable—it cannot be seen or experienced through the senses. According to Laozi, people become separated from Tao when the wrong things become important to them, such as power, success, and learning. When people abandon those things, they will be enriched in spirit. Ambition and contention block "quietism" and the ability to open oneself to unity with Tao.

Zhuangzi

The *Tao Te Ching* was written as an aid to kingship. In addition to the passages on how to live and how to find Tao, it contained many sections on how to govern. As we said earlier, it was written for a ruler, not for the common people. Thus, the first people who followed Laozi's teachings were mainly those from the ruling families, those who had access to education. Some of those early followers may have traveled to the hills to become hermits and to commune with nature as Laozi himself presumably did at the end of his life. But those who adopted Laozi's teachings did so as a personal philosophy, which they practiced privately.

About two centuries after Laozi, another great Taoist master emerged. His name was Zhuangzi (Chuang Tzu), and he lived from about 369 to 286 B.C.E. He became known as the next great Taoist sage and one of the great literary figures of Chinese history. The *Zhuangzi*, the collection of the works of Master Zhuang, was the first Chinese work to present a philosophy of life that ordinary people could understand and follow for themselves.

Like the *Tao Te Ching*, the *Zhuangzi* may have been written by more than one person or even collected by others after Zhuangzi's death. Nevertheless, tradition has it that the works in the book are his. Zhuangzi was a scholar who had studied the works of Laozi. He wrote essays, stories, and parables to illustrate and explain Laozi's teachings to others. Zhuangzi's message is much like that of Laozi, but his style is very different. Instead of short, compact sayings about life and its meaning, Zhuangzi wrote chatty stories that ordinary people could relate to easily. His pages illustrate the sayings of Laozi with characters who not only are kings and sages but also are ordinary Chinese working-class potters and meat-cutters. Zhuangzi did a great deal to spread awareness of Taoism to the common folk of China.

In his writings, Zhuangzi rejected political and social concerns. He believed that living within ordinary society made people forget Tao, or the ultimate reality. Society, he suggested, caused people to become obsessed with tasks, routines, successes—all the things that stand in the way of true success—and to lose contact with the simple life of union with Tao, which is at the root of their being.

In a time when Confucian scholar-officials were finding favor in the emperor's court, Zhuangzi remained cheerfully scornful of government. He said that someone who served the state was like a bejeweled tortoise kept by the emperor in a silk-lined box. He himself, he explained, would far rather be like the live tortoise basking in the sun on the riverbank or floating in muddy water, happy and free in its natural state.

Zhuangzi took Laozi's abstract ideas and applied them to concrete, everyday situations. What could Laozi have meant when he wrote, "The world is won by those who let it go"? In explanation, Zhuangzi wrote:

When an archer is shooting for nothing,
He has all his skill.
If he shoots for a brass buckle
He is already nervous.
If he shoots for a prize of gold
He goes blank or sees two targets—
He is out of his mind!
His skill has not changed.
But the prize divides him. He cares.
He thinks more of winning
Than of shooting—
And the need to win
Drains him of power.

Here was something everyone could understand. Who has never had the experience of doing well in rehearsal and poorly in performance? Zhuangzi's message was that outside concerns distract people from being their best. It is necessary to give up the desire to win in order to win. Things should be done for their own sake and not for some other gain.

In another of his writings, Zhuangzi explained Laozi's teachings about achieving mastery or perfection. Here is his tale of a master carver who sought harmony with the universe before beginning his work with the wood.

Khing, the master carver, made a bell stand
Of precious wood. When it was finished,
All who saw it were astounded. They said it must be
The work of spirits.

The Prince of Lu said to the master carver:
"What is your secret?"
Khing replied: "I am only a workman:
I have no secret. There is only this:
When I began to think about the work you commanded
I guarded my spirit, did not expend it
On trifles, that were not to the point.
I fasted in order to set
My heart at rest.

After three days fasting,
I had forgotten gain and success.
After five days
I had forgotten praise or criticism.
After seven days,
I had forgotten my body
With all its limbs.

"By this time all thought of your Highness
And of the court had faded away.
All that might distract me from the work
Had vanished.
I was collected in the single thought
Of the bell stand.
Then I went to the forest
To see the trees in their own natural state.
When the right tree appeared before my eyes,
The bell stand also appeared in it, clearly, beyond doubt.

"All I had to do was to put forth my hand
And begin.

"If I had not met this particular tree
There would have been
No bell stand at all.

"What happened?
My own collected thought
Encountered the hidden potential in the wood;
From this live encounter came the work
Which you ascribe to the spirits."

The master carver achieved mastery of his art by ignoring all thought of gain or praise or even of his own skill. He came into harmony with the tree and, therefore, with the natural universe, the ultimate reality that is Tao.

The Tao concept of wuwei, or "non-doing," Zhuangzi explained this way:

Here is how I sum it up:
Heaven does nothing: its non-doing is its serenity.

Earth does nothing: its non-doing is its rest.
From the union of these two non-doings
All actions proceed,
All things are made.
How vast, how invisible
This coming-to-be!
All things come from nowhere!
No way to explain it!
All beings in their perfection
Are born of non-doing.
"Hence it is said:
Heaven and earth do nothing
Yet there is nothing they do not do.
Where is the man who can attain
   to this non-doing?

As Zhuangzi explained it, the philosophy of non-doing does not mean withdrawing from action but rather performing a higher kind of action: action in accord with Tao, action that respects the nature of all things.

During Zhuangzi's lifetime, the Zhou dynasty was beset by wars and conflict. It finally fell to the brief rule of the Qin (Ch'in) dynasty in 221 B.C.E. In 202 B.C.E., yet another dynasty came into power.

The Han dynasty, which would reign until 220 C.E., eventually adopted Confucianism as the basis of state government. At the beginning, though, the rulers followed Taoist principles. They tried to interfere as little as possible with the lives of the citizens in order to allow them to recover from the years of bloodshed and war. During that time, a number of Taoist sages studied Laozi and Zhuangzi and wrote commentaries on their work.

Li An and the Huainan Masters

Liu An (d. 122 B.C.E.) was the grandson of the first emperor of the Han dynasty and was the the king of Huainan, a minor Chinese kingdom. He invited scholars and wise men from all over the empire to come to his court, and he made it a center of learning in the arts and sciences.

According to legend, a group of eight Taoist wise men appeared at Liu An's court, seeking to join the hundreds of scholars already at work there. The king, perhaps feeling that he already had enough wise men, asked the Taoists to prove that they had something new to offer. They so dazzled the king with their knowledge and skill that he begged them to let him become their apprentice. Their lectures and lessons are recorded in a series of essays that became the third great Taoist classic text, the *Huainanzi*, or "Masters of Huainan."

This book is a collection of twenty-one essays. It is not purely Taoist, as it incorporates some Confucian methods of self-improvement. This blending of philosophies may actually have helped Taoism survive as a popular movement, because it served as a bridge between followers of Confucianism and the mystical ideas of Laozi.

The *Huainanzi* quotes extensively from the *Tao Te Ching*. Thus, although an important work in its own right, it also helped to preserve the text of Laozi's work and guarantee its influence.

One of Liu An's interests was alchemy, an offshoot of Taoist medical arts. The alchemists experimented with all kinds of magical spells and common materials—animal, vegetable, and mineral—as they tried to find a way to turn those common materials into gold. The goal of alchemy was not to create wealth, but to produce a formula for a golden potion—the so-called "elixir of life"—that would ensure immortality and everlasting youth.

In China, there had long been magicians, or "wonder workers," people who offered charms and secret words to ward off evil spirits and summon up good ones. These magicians were attracted to Taoist writings because they felt that many of them hinted at magical wonders. The *Zhuangzi* did include references to "supreme men," or immortals, who could pass through water without getting wet and through fire without getting burned. Those passages captured the imagination of many early followers of Taoism.

Around the fourth century B.C.E., Taoist scholars assembled a book called *The Yellow Emperor's Classic of Internal Medicine*, named for Huang Di, the great ancestor in the Taoist tradition. The book's first chapter discussed ways to achieve immortality and long life. Many people came to believe that there must be a practical way to become immortal. Alchemists set about trying to find the specific formula for immortality. No alchemist ever found it, but emperors and kings never stopped desiring it and the alchemists never stopped pursuing it.

The path to immortality was a long and complicated process. It was necessary to achieve total physical and spiritual harmony through meditation, diet, exercise, breath control, the use of herbs, and other special practices. All disease had to be eliminated from the body and all evil eliminated from the spirit. The final step was to swallow the alchemical "golden potion." Although the elixir of life was known to be supremely dangerous for the imperfectly prepared person, it was believed that it would not harm anyone who had achieved earthly perfection. Indeed, no one could become immortal without taking the potion.

■ *A woman in southern Taiwan sells a preparation to help increase longevity, long an important aspect of Taoist practice.*

While hunting for this magical elixir, the Taoist sages discovered many anesthetics and medicines. By learning how metals combined through heat, they developed gunpowder and invented fireworks. They created chemical dyes and pigments, as well as the glazes that make Chinese porcelain so beautiful. The understanding they gained of practical chemistry far exceeded that of any other culture at that time.

Liu An's court may have included hundreds of scientists who worked as alchemists and, by chance, made discoveries that furthered both science and medicine. Among their discoveries was a way to convert soy beans into bean curd, or tofu. While this food product did not prove to be the elixir of life, it did provide a valuable form of vegetable protein for people in a land where there was never enough meat. It also made the killing of animals unnecessary, thus contributing to Taoist principles.

Before the *Huainanzi* became well known in the empire, however, political turmoil caused Liu An's downfall. He disappeared and the masters scattered. Soon after, Confucianism became the official state system of thought and education throughout the empire.

Temporarily, Taoism was repressed. It remained alive, however, mainly as a matter of private interest among some of the more adventurous Confucians and still fewer pure Taoists. Yet Liu An's book contributed to a growing body of Taoist literature that continued to influence Chinese scholars and thinkers.

CHAPTER 3

The Growth
and Spread of
Religious Taoism

*T*he history of Taoism is one of political ups and downs. Taoists either enjoyed considerable favor or had almost none at all. More often than not, they were out of favor or at least observed with disapproval by the more conservative bureaucratic Confucians.

In the *Tao Te Ching*, Laozi had formulated a philosophy of government. "Governing a large country is like frying a small fish," he wrote. "You spoil it with too much poking." He advised rulers to fix their minds on Tao and stop meddling; later Taoists, such as Zhuangzi, developed this attitude even further. On the whole, Taoists were not so much against government as above it. They were supremely disinterested. They preferred fishing in a mountain stream to shuffling papers in the imperial court.

Throughout history, Taoism flourished in times of weak government and political chaos. Strong emperors, unless they were very secure and tolerant, tended to take a dim view of an organization that preached anarchy—the concept that the best government was no government at all. Given a choice between the hard-working, rule-following Confucians or the Taoists with their

minds turned toward nature and finding the Tao, the emperors usually chose Confucians. There were Taoists in most imperial courts, but they were engaged in alchemy, not government.

Taoists had a reputation for rebelliousness. They saw no conflict between their philosophy and fighting—there was almost always a war being waged in China, either internally or against invaders. War was a way of life recognized in the *Tao Te Ching*. Laozi said, "In war, those who regard it as lamentable but necessary will win." Taoists studied swordplay and martial arts as part of their devotional practice. They elevated defense to a high art. Some of China's greatest military strategists were Taoists.

Emperors often regarded the Taoists, with their lack of respect for orderly government, as impudent and perhaps dangerous. From time to time, a Taoist group would become powerful enough to seem a threat. Then Taoism was suppressed, usually brutally. Suppression in imperial China often meant that Taoist leaders paid with their heads.

Being a Taoist was risky. Even in the best of times, political favor was unlikely to last. Taoism survived as a largely underground movement, attracting the disenchanted, the unsuccessful, and the disenfranchised. But survive it did, because it tapped something deep in the Chinese consciousness.

The Seeds of Religious Taoism

Laozi, Zhuangzi, and the other early Taoist sages meant their writings as practical guides for living. They were not thinking about starting a religion as Buddha did, nor were they consciously working to reform an existing religion as Jesus did. These early Taoist sages drew their ideas at least in part from ancient Chinese religious traditions, but their aim was to record their philosophy, their thoughts on society and government and the human condition. Their ideas are known as *Tao jia*—"Taoist thought," or the philosophy of Taoism.

Taoism's early followers were mostly people who searched individually for Tao. Some became deeply immersed in the alchemical or the governmental aspects of Tao. These followers attached themselves to imperial courts, where they amazed or

> ■ **The Journey of a Thousand Miles**
>
> Prevent trouble before it arises.
>
> Put things in order before they exist.
>
> The giant pine tree grows from a tiny sprout.
>
> The journey of a thousand miles starts from beneath your feet.
>
> —from the **Tao Te Ching**

advised emperors. Others withdrew from society altogether and became hermits, communing with nature deep in the mountains. Early Taoists in general had little interest in forming an organized religion.

By the time of the Han dynasty, however, some of the Taoist sages were attracting a following. The Confucian-based government no longer seemed to be working. People who were looking for an alternative found it in the *Tao Te Ching.*

The Way of Great Peace

One of the central themes of the *Tao Te Ching* is government. Laozi had described a society in which all people worked together in harmony and contentment, with little governmental interference. The *Zhuangzi* related this governmental ideal to the legendary rule of the Yellow Emperor and to other great sage-emperors thousands of years earlier. Confucian texts, too, glorified this ancient time called the *Taiping,* or "Great Peace."

These texts inspired the dream of a utopia, a perfect society. In the second century, the dream became a popular movement in the eastern provinces under the leadership of a Taoist named Zhang Zhue (Chang Chueh).

Zhang Zhue hoped to create a society in which the search for Tao would be the supreme goal. His society would center on the pursuit of Tao, and everyone would live according to Taoist principles. The *Tao Te Ching* of Laozi would serve as a guidebook to the art of perfect government.

Zhang Zhue foretold ten years of political disasters and natural catastrophes. He promised, however, to protect those who followed him and repented of their sins. The Han rulers were weak and corrupt, and people could easily imagine the troubles Zhang Zhue predicted. His vision of a serene and peaceful government appealed to them. His movement became immensely popular.

In 184 C.E., Zhang Zhue announced that the "blue heaven" of the Han dynasty, which came from the east where blue-green was the symbolic color, was to be replaced by the "yellow heaven" of his perfect society. The Chinese character for *blue* also stood for *old,* a reference to the old and now corrupt eastern Han rule.

■ *This silk tapestry depicts a scene of the Taoist paradise. In the sky is the Queen of the Western Heavens with her attendants. Nearest her, at the railing, stand the three gods of longevity, prosperity, and happiness. Descending the staircase are the Eight Immortals. At the top, Han Zhung Li holds a fan. A little below him stands Lu Dongbin with his sword. At the bottom are Di Kuai Li with his crutch, Han Xiang Zi with his flute, and Ho Xian Ku with her lotus flower.*

Yellow was the color of the central districts of China, from which Zhang Zhue came. His followers, by now over two hundred thousand strong, wore yellow turbans. They worshiped Huang Lao—a deity whose name was a combination of the names of Huang Di (the Yellow Emperor) and Laozi.

Under the slogan "The Blue Heaven has died and the Yellow Heaven is coming to Power," the Yellow Turbans rose in revolt against the government. Mobs burned towns and ransacked the homes of the ruling classes. Eventually, the superior army of the Han dynasty put down the rebellion, and the survivors scattered. Some fled to the north, where they joined a Taoist movement that had already begun there. The Yellow Turban revolt was the first of many similar rebellions with Taoist elements that occurred throughout history, often in times of foreign occupation.

Taoism Becomes a Religion

The first Buddhist missionaries had come to China from India before the common era. As time went on, they steadily became more active in winning converts. Buddhism was an attractive religion, and by the first century C.E., it was spreading rapidly. It was not Chinese, however. Although many people were dissatisfied with ethical, rule-oriented Confucianism, they clung to the Chinese folk religions. Like Buddhism, those ancient religions featured many gods, along with ghosts, demons, and evil spirits.

Beginning in the second century, Taoism in the northern provinces of China began to change in the hands of a man named Zhang Dao Ling (Chang Tao Ling), whose family had been Taoists and alchemists for generations. Zhang saw the growing influence of Buddhism. He understood that Buddhism was spreading in China, in part because it had many gods and goddesses and magical rituals, similar to the ancient Chinese folk religions. Buddhism was not as abstract as Taoism was. It was not based mainly on a code of ethics as was Confucianism. It offered the spiritual comfort of ritual and close contact with gods who could influence daily life.

It is said that in the year 142, the spirit of Laozi, now a god in heaven, appeared to Zhang Dao Ling. The immortal spirit of

Laozi gave Zhang Dao Ling the authority to establish a religion, a specific system of beliefs and worship, that would replace the many folk religions with one based on Taoist principles.

Under Zhang, Taoism acquired a new set of characteristics, including the belief in many gods and goddesses, the practice of casting magical spells, and the institution of a set of rituals to be followed. In some ways, this new religion was like Buddhism. Its character, however, was decidedly Chinese. For his new faith, Zhang established a religious organization with a hierarchy of spiritual leaders. He drew together many elements into a coherent whole. Because of this, he is credited with being the founder of *Tao jiao*, religious Taoism.

■ *Chinese Names*

Because there are two alphabet systems for spelling Chinese words in English, names and titles that appear in this book may have a different form in reference works, library catalogues, and other literature. People's names are written with the family name first; pronunciation is the same for both spellings. Some equivalents appear below:

Pinyin Form	**Wade–Giles or Other Form**
Dao, Daoism	Tao, Taoism
Daodejing	**Tao Te Ching**
Qing dynasty	Ch'in (or) Ching dynasty
Tang dynasty	T'ang dynasty
Song dynasty	Sung dynasty
Zhou dynasty	Chou dynasty
Huang Di (the Yellow Emperor)	Huang Ti, Hwang Ti
Laozi	Lao Tzu, Lao Tze
Zhang Dao Ling	Chang Tao Ling
Zhuangzi (or) Zhuang Zhou	Chuang Tzu (or) Chuang Chou
Li Bai (or) Li Bo	Li Po
Cao Cao	Ts'ao Ts'ao
taijiquan	t'ai chi ch'uan
Quanzhen (Highest Purity)	Ch'uan Chen
Yijing (Book of Changes)	**I Ching**
Ba Xian (the Eight Immortals)	Pa Hsien

The Way of the Celestial Masters

Zhang Dao Ling called his movement *Tien Shi*, or "Way of the Celestial Masters." He himself became the first celestial master, taking his authority from *Tai shang Lao jun*, which means "Divine Lord Lao"—that is, Laozi. Under Zhang Dao Ling, the *Tao Te Ching* came to be viewed as a divinely revealed book because it was the work of the deified Laozi.

Zhang Dao Ling became known as a healer. He connected sickness with sin, either one's own sin or the sin of an ancestor. He devised rituals to cleanse people of their sins and heal them. Those seeking healing would write their sins on a piece of paper and wade into a river, holding the paper above their heads, until their sins were washed away. Thus, Zhang offered not only physical cures, but also spiritual and psychological healing. Through the Taoism of Zhang Dao Ling, an ordinary person might hope for salvation.

Zhang traveled the countryside, casting out demons and curing diseases. As an alchemist, he had knowledge and skill that few people possessed. He achieved some miraculous cures, drawing many converts to the new faith.

The Rise of Taocracy

Other Taoist masters had gathered followers, but Zhang drew his into an organization divided into twenty-four units, or parishes, each centered on a place of worship called an oratory. The oratory was overseen by a priest called a libationer, to whom Zhang delegated ritual powers. When a follower brought a problem or a wish to the libationer, it was the libationer's duty to determine which of the many Taoist gods and spirits should be petitioned to deal with it and to send it on the appropriate way. There were three Taoist heavens, each one higher than the last, and each with many sections, not unlike the government of a large Chinese city of the time. Indeed, the Taoist heavens are often referred to as the "heavenly bureaucracy."

Once a petition reached the proper heavenly department, the official gods of that precinct would hear it and rule on its merit. Then, if they chose, they could summon the necessary heavenly forces against the demon causing the trouble.

Members of the community also met to celebrate feasts in which the sharing of food was a communion with Tao. In addition to regularly scheduled feast times, community members met to celebrate religious occasions and for other group activities. Their community activities helped to keep them together as a group and to keep the Taocracy functioning.

To support the system, the Taoist organization taxed each household five pecks of rice. Because of this tax, Zhang's movement was mocked by the Confucianists as the Way of the Five Pecks of Rice (instead of Way of the Celestial Masters). But the movement was strong, both religiously and politically. Its strength may even have contributed to the Han dynasty's ultimate downfall.

Zhang Dao Ling is said to have received a sword and a seal from heaven. With these, and with magic charms he had received from Laozi, he was able to capture and slay demons. At the end of his earthly life, Zhang Dao Ling became immortal, and the sword passed to his descendents for their use in protecting the people from evil. His son Zhang Heng and then his grandson Zhang Lu took over the leadership of the celestial masters, establishing a line of spiritual leaders who are often referred to as the popes of Taoism.

With the Han dynasty failing, the well-organized Way of the Celestial Masters gained substantial political power. Zhang Lu was able to set up a small, independent, religion-centered state in what is now Shanxi Province in eastern China. Under his rule, inns were constructed that would be free for travelers, alcoholic beverages were banned, new roads were built, and food banks were established to feed the poor. Zhang Lu established a system of justice that featured rehabilitation of criminals through faith and kindness. On the whole, life in the Taocracy was substantially better than life in much of imperial China.

In spite of the turmoil in China as the Han dynasty came apart, the Taocracy of the Zhang family lasted thirty years. Then in 215, Zhang Lu agreed to submit to the authority of a Han general, Cao Cao (Ts'ao Ts'ao), whose forces had subdued the surrounding territory. Only six years later, China split into three states: Wei, Shu, and Wu. Cao Cao became the founder of the Wei dynasty, which lay in the north. He formally recognized the sect of the celestial masters. They, in turn, agreed to support the government, as long as it was run on Taoist principles. The arrangement proved to be mutually beneficial, and the Way of the Celestial Masters continued to win followers in the courts of the Wei rulers throughout the third century.

Taoism in the South

Early in the fourth century C.E., northern China was invaded by various nomadic tribes that came sweeping in on horseback from Manchuria, Mongolia, Tibet, and other lands farther to the north. Many of the celestial masters migrated to the south.

Other Taoists had been there before them. The most influential was Go Hong (Ko Hung) (283–343 C.E.), a student of Taoist philosophy and alchemy. He had an active career in government and the military and also managed to write widely on many topics. His book *Baopuzi*, or "He Who Holds to Simplicity," attempted to draw together Confucian ethics and Taoist beliefs. The *Baopuzi* is one of the earliest and most complete descriptions of the alchemists' search for the elixir of life. It explained Taoist belief in immortality and developed the idea of working toward "spiritual alchemy," or perfection without alchemical formulas. Finally, it established a merit system for doing good works as a necessary part of achieving immortal life. A charismatic leader, Go Hong helped to prepare the way for the new religion to take hold.

Arriving in the southeast from the war-torn north, the celestial masters began an active campaign to win people away from the old folk religions and over to Taoism. They succeeded in attracting converts from many of the aristocratic families in the region, and their numbers grew steadily. But their form of Taoism was about to change once again.

The Highest Purity Sect

Beginning in 364, a Taoist named Yang Xi (Yang Hsi), an official in the imperial court, had a series of visions. In those visions, which lasted until 370, he saw a group of immortals, people who had achieved spiritual and physical perfection and

■ *A Taoist priest in rich ceremonial robes holds a wand as a symbol of his position. The rustic staff behind him and the platform on which he sits suggest the close tie between Taoism and the natural world.*

had been taken up into the Highest Purity Heaven of the Taoists. They revealed to him a whole new body of scripture and much practical information. The immortals are said to have told Yang Xi that the period in which he was living, marked by war, disease, and the worship of false gods, would end in fire and flood and would be replaced by a rule of Tao.

Yang Xi saw that to bring about the rule of Tao in the south, the northern Way of the Celestial Masters would have to adapt to southern ways. He set about making the necessary reforms. Yang Xi's genius enabled him to bring together elements of Buddhism and local religions, along with traditional Taoist beliefs. He transformed and reshaped many elements of Taoism. His transformations came to be called both the Highest Purity movement and the Mao Shan school, named for Mount Mao where it was founded. Mao Shan, one of the five mountains sacred to Taoism, rises south of the Yangtze River near Shanghai and Nanking.

The Highest Purity Taoists greatly enriched the practices and rituals of the Way of the Celestial Masters and strengthened Taoism. The Highest Purity Taoists emphasized the use of meditation and withdrawal from the world to allow a return to the "pure" principles of Taoism. This movement also produced a number of exceptional thinkers, one of whom was Dao Hong Jing (Tao Hung Ching) (456–536), who became the foremost Taoist master of his time. He emphasized the importance of wuwei, the emptying of the mind of all thought so that Tao might enter.

Like many of the Taoist masters, Dao Hong Jing was a man of vast energy and many talents. A poet, a master of calligraphy (the art of Chinese handwriting), and a student of natural history, Dao Hong Jing is also remembered as the founder of pharmacology, or the study of the qualities, uses, and preparation of drugs in medicine. He edited and annotated the manuscripts of Yang Xi on which the Highest Purity movement was based. He withdrew to Mao Shan, where he sought to live and work entirely according to Tao. A number of followers lived with him there under his spiritual guidance.

Dao Hong Jing was a close friend of Emperor Wu Di of the Liang dynasty (502–556). The Wu emperor had been a Taoist in his youth, but he later became a fervent Buddhist. In 504, the emperor banned all Taoist groups. However, he honored his close friendship with Dao Hong Jing and he and his followers were allowed to continue their work, thus preserving the community of Taoists at Mao Shan. Dao Hong Jing's influence is still felt among Mao Shan Taoists. From his teachings, his disciple Wang Yuanji (Wang Yuan Chi) created liturgies and rituals of great beauty and appeal that are still being used and which continue to attract people to Taoism.

Other Taoist movements developed in the south. Their leaders, like those of the Highest Purity movement, tried to adapt Taoism into a dynamic, popular religion. Among all of the groups, however, the Highest Purity Taoists founded by Yang Xi remained the most prominent form of Taoism in the south.

Taoism in the North

In the north, meanwhile, the Way of the Celestial Masters was undergoing a rebirth. In 415, Kou Zhen Qi (K'ou Chen Chi) had a visitation from Divine Lord Lao (Laozi) in which Lao named him Celestial Master and instructed him to reform Taoism. Kou set out to bring the Way of the Celestial Masters into line with the writings of Laozi. He denounced certain practices, such as the tax of five pecks of rice, as corrupt and corrupting. "What have such matters to do with the pure Tao?" he cried angrily.

Kou's proposed reforms won the attention—and the favor—of the Wei emperor Tai Wu Di, who gave him power over all religious practices of the state and proclaimed Taoism the official religion of the empire. In return, Kou gave the emperor a Taoist insignia, designating him the earthly representative of Divine Lord Lao on earth. Thus, in the north and throughout China, Taoism continued to have an influence on Chinese government and cultural life.

Taoism Under the Tang Emperors

In 618, a new dynasty came into power, finally bringing peace. Under the Tang emperors, China was once again unified. The Tang dynasty would rule China until 907, almost three hundred years. Their rule was marked by great achievements in poetry, sculpture, painting, and scholarship.

The official religion of the Tang state was Confucianism, but the founder of the dynasty was Li Yuan, who traced his ancestry back to Li Ehr, or Laozi himself. Under the leadership of Li Yuan and those of his descendants, Taoism won increasing favor. Although it again did not become the official state religion, it had the government's respect.

■ *The Hundred-Character Tablet of Lu Yan*
Nurturing energy, forget words and guard it.
Conquer the mind, do non-doing.
In activity and quietude, know the source progenitor.
There is no thing; whom else do you seek?
Real constancy should respond to people;
In responding to people, it is essential not to get confused.
When you don't get confused, your nature is naturally stable;
    when your nature is stable, energy naturally returns.
When energy returns, elixir spontaneously crystalizes,
    in the pot pairing water and fire.
Yin and yang arise, alternating over and over again,
    everywhere producing the sound of thunder.
White clouds assemble on the summit,
    sweet dew bathes the polar mountain.
Having drunk the wine of longevity,
    you wander free; who can know you?
You sit and listen to the stringless tune,
You clearly understand the mechanism of creation.
The whole of these twenty verses
Is a ladder straight to heaven.
—from **Vitality, Energy, Spirit: A Taoist Sourcebook,** translated
and edited by Thomas Cleary

The Mao Shan, or Highest Purity Taoists, were the dominant religious group of the time. The most famous Highest Purity Taoist of the Tang era was Su-ma Cheng-zhen (Ssu-ma Ch'eng-chen) (647–735). He became the spiritual master to emperors, and his treatise on meditation became a classic.

Under the Tangs, the *Tao Te Ching* increased in importance as a sacred work, and every family in the empire was required to have a copy. Meditation, alchemy, and magic were popular. Laozi's birthday became a national holiday, and the dynasty built Taoist temples and monasteries at Mount Mao and Mount Song. Taoist literature spread throughout the empire and across the borders into Tibet and India.

Taoism and the Song Dynasty

The fall of the Tang dynasty in 907 ushered in a period of warfare and political confusion that ended when the Song dynasty (960–1279) emerged. Under Song emperors, Taoism again became the official state religion. The Song rulers officially recognized the claim of the leaders of Highest Purity Taoism that their lineage back to Zhang Dao Ling, the founder of religious Taoism, was unbroken.

By this time, Taoist masters had come to realize that there was no golden elixir of life. During the Mao Shan revelations, the immortals who appeared to Yang Xi had given him formulas for elixirs that they said were their food and drink. They cautioned, however, that these elixirs would be deadly poisonous to mortals. The search for alchemical gold was officially discouraged. While still teaching techniques of longevity and spiritual improvement, Taoist masters rejected the notion of a chemical elixir. Alchemy came to be understood as spiritual, a blend of the elements of body, mind, and spirit into a harmonious whole.

Immortality, though, remained a major concern of Taoism. Among the common people, a tradition was evolving concerning a class of heavenly beings known as immortals. For people who had practiced a folk religion before coming to Taoism, the spirit world was more real than the emperor's court. The immortals were folk heroes, in some cases historically well-known people who were believed to have achieved physical as well as spiritual immortality, often through suffering. They would appear in ordinary society from time to time, do good works (or create mischief for evil-doers), and then be assumed into heaven once again. The immortals came to occupy an important place, much like that of Christian saints.

The Song emperor Zhen Cong (Chen Tsung) (998–1020), a Taoist, added to the hosts of heaven by declaring additional gods and immortals and giving them ranks in the heavenly hierarchy. The god known as the Jade Emperor had the most powerful position, ruling as he did over the gods of earth and water and such immortals as Laozi and the Yellow Emperor. These heavenly folk waged a continual battle against the evil spirits and demons in the Ten Courts of the Underworld.

In the Song period, temples and monasteries were established in every province. In 1015, the emperor granted the celestial masters a large area of land at Lung Hu Shan, or Dragon-Tiger Mountain in what is now Jiangxi (Kiangsi) Province in southeastern China. This was to be their stronghold until they were driven out by the Chinese Communists in 1930. Under the Song emperors, many Taoist works were collected, and an encyclopedia was compiled to preserve early Taoist writings.

Printing had become widespread in China, and in 1016 the emperor supported the printing of the Taoist *Canon*, the *Tao Ts'ang (Daocang)*, the collected works that were the main resource of the Taoist religion. Taoism was now dominated by the two organizations that had stood the test of time—the Highest Purity movement and the Way of the Celestial Masters.

The Complete Reality Sect

In 1126, a wave of Tartar invaders came down from the north, toppling the Song emperor. A Song prince escaped and set up a new government along Confucian lines. Confucianism, however, had changed. Influenced by Taoism, Confucian thinkers began to consider for the first time the philosophical questions of being and other problems of human existence.

In the south, Taoism was repressed. In the occupied north, however, new Taoist groups sprang up. The strongest of these groups was the Complete Reality movement *(Quanzhen)*, a revival movement founded by Wang Zhong-yang (Wang Chung-yang) (1113–1170).

The Complete Reality movement was marked by a return to naturalness and freedom that had characterized ancient Taoism. Its leaders recommended "clear serenity" for their followers. They

千峰山暝
盃向䫂蕴、
舉堂寒色
真前屋把
書字不輓
斯人庶是
友松人
南陵仰順

■ *Taoism strongly influenced Chinese landscape painting. This handscroll, "Wind and Snow in the Fir-Pines" by Li Shan, a Qin dynasty artist, is typical in its use of strong natural forms, like tall trees and towering mountain peaks. The lone figure of the scholar, dwarfed by the natural setting, suggests the relative unimportance of human beings in the Taoist universe.*

traced their branch of thought back to Lu Yan, a Taoist of the Tang era who became known as Ancestor Lu. A Confucian scholar, Lu Yan came to Taoism in middle age. According to belief, he became immortal in body as well as spirit; he reappears in times of trouble to help those who call on his power. Lu Yan left behind a body of writing that integrated Buddhist and Confucianist thought with philosophical, religious, and alchemical Taoism. Later, Complete Reality Taoists built increasingly on this blending of traditions.

The Complete Reality Taoists attracted the attention of the Mongol rulers of the north. The famous Mongol conqueror Genghis Khan invited Wang's successor, Qiu Zhang-jun (Ch'iu Chang Chun) (1148–1227), to come to his court and preach. Genghis Khan asked Qiu for the elixir of life, but the master would offer only Taoist principles of health and serenity. Nevertheless, Genghis Khan looked kindly on the Taoists, and through Qui's efforts, Taoists were permitted to continue to worship freely.

■ Later Chinese Dynasties

Eastern Han Dynasty (25–220)
Fine paper produced (105)
Silk Road developed for trade throughout Asia
Yellow Turban Rebellion (184)

Three Kingdoms Dynasty (220–265)
Shu, Wei, Wu kingdoms established
Rise of Buddhism
Increasing importance of Taoism

Jin Dynasty (265–589)
Increased influence of Buddhism
Invasions from the North (early 4th century)

Sui Dynasty (590–618)
China reunified (589)
Buddhism and Taoism favored
Canal system established
Confucian system of civil service examinations introduced

Tang Dynasty (618–906)
Great achievements in poetry, sculpture, painting
Rise of scholar-officials in government
Territorial expansion

Five Dynasties (907–960)
China divided into independent kingdoms
Non-Chinese control North China
First military use of gunpowder

Song Dynasty (960–1279)
China reunified
Great age of landscape painting
Neo-Confucianism dominates
Genghis Khan conquers North China (1167–1227)
Period of warfare with Mongols

Yuan Dynasty (1279–1368)
Mongol dynasty established by Kublai Khan
Growing contact with the West; visits of Marco Polo
Confucianism, Taoism discouraged

Ming Dynasty (1368–1644)
Mongols expelled
Civil service examinations and Confucianism reinstated
European traders and missionaries in China

Qing Dynasty (1644–1911)
Established by Manchus
European influence grows
Chinese power weakens
Dynastic rule ends

Reversals Under the Yuan Dynasty

Genghis Khan's grandson, Kublai Khan, was less benevolent than his grandfather. Kublai Khan made Buddhism the official religion of his Yuan dynasty, which ruled China from 1279 to 1368, and he commanded that almost all Taoist books be seized and burned. He allowed only the *Tao Te Ching* and Taoist books on medicine, pharmacy, and science to be preserved.

As a result of Kublai Khan's decree, Taoist literature dating back over ten centuries was destroyed. Taoism, however, could not be wiped out; instead, it went underground. All across China, Taoism's followers saved what literature they could, and what they could not save, they kept alive in the oral tradition.

Revolts in South China and Mongolia weakened the rule of the Kublai Khan. In 1368, a leader named Chu Yuan-zhang drove the Mongols out of Peking (now Beijing) and seized power, establishing the Ming dynasty (1368–1644). By 1382, the last of the Mongol invaders were driven out of China, and peace returned.

Taoism Under the Mings

Under Ming rule, the native culture of the Chinese people was restored. The government enacted a new code of law, free of all Mongol elements and practices. Walls, temples, shrines, highways, and gardens were rebuilt. At the direction of the Ming emperor, scholars began compiling a collection of the best of Chinese literature and thought. Although the first emperor was Buddhist, he was tolerant of all of China's religions. He promoted Confucianism for the state, but encouraged other faiths as well. The result was a renewed interest in Taoism and Buddhism among the common people and a surge in religious learning among scholars. Between 1506 and 1521, Taoist scholars published a body of writings that they had been assembling for seventy years. Their commentaries promoted a return to earlier Taoist principles, which they saw as a purer form of Taoism.

One of the important figures of the Ming period was Zhang San Feng, who in Taoist lore is said to have achieved immortality and to have reappeared after death. Like many of the semi-legendary masters, he lived an exceptionally long life. Some sources claim that he was born under the Song dynasty (960–1279); others claim that he lived during the Yuan dynasty (1279–1368). But it is known that a Taoist sage by that name was summoned to the Ming court in the fifteenth century. Perhaps there was more than one Taoist with that name.

Whenever he lived and whoever he was, Zhang San Feng left behind a large body of writing on Taoist themes, including commentaries on the works of Ancestor Lu. He drew together the thinking of both northern and southern Taoism, along with magical elements from still earlier times. Zhang's varied subjects showed his wide-ranging interests and intellect. His essay on human character explains how many types of personality—lazy or energetic, quick or slow, meek or warlike—may be seen as being in harmony with Tao. He also wrote about medicine and the importance of treating others with love.

Zhang San Feng emphasized the interaction of mind and body in the art of meditation. This interaction is perhaps the reason that Zhang San Feng is remembered as the founder of taijiquan, the system of devotional exercise practiced by Taoist masters to free and cleanse the body so that the mind may be at ease.

The Qing Dynasty

In 1644, after many years of warfare, an army from Manchuria, northeast of China, swept into Peking and conquered it. These peoples, the Manchus, established the Qing (Ching) dynasty (1644–1911), which would be the last dynasty of China.

Although they spoke a different language and came from a different background, the Manchus left the customs of the Ming government fairly intact. They made few major changes in Chinese society or in the economy, and they took a lenient attitude toward religion. One of the changes they did make was to require Chinese men to adopt Manchu clothes and to wear their hair long in a pigtail, or braid, as a sign of submission. Taoist priests, however, were exempt from these requirements.

By the sixteenth century, Taoist experimentation with minerals, plants, and animals—part of the search for good health and the elixir of life—had produced fifty-two chapters on medicinal drugs, together known as the *Great Pharmacopoeia*. This volume demonstrated once again Taoism's effect on science and medicine. Throughout the Qing period, individual Taoist masters, like Liu Yi-ming (ca. 1737–1826) continued to study ancient works and to write commentaries on them. One of his most famous treatises explained the *Yijing (I Ching),* one of the ancient Chinese *Five Classics* and a book of prophecy and wisdom that dates to the century before Confucius. Translated into English by a contemporary scholar in the early nineteenth century, it was one of the first volumes to make Chinese thought accessible to the West.

As early as the Tang period, attempts were made to fuse Taoism, Confucianism, and Chinese Buddhism into one religion, all of which met with varying success. One of those movements was the Great Success movement, or *Da Cheng Jiao (Ta Ch'eng Chiao).* Begun by Li Zhao En (Lee Chao En) during the Ming period, it was heavily Confucian but it incorporated aspects of all three faiths. Generally, Buddhists and Confucianists kept to their own ways, but many Taoists adopted the fusion viewpoint. By the time of the Qing dynasty, as many as ten thousand followers would meet to read from the *Da Xue (Ta Hsueh),* or "Great Learning," which merged the three great traditions of China.

Yet Taoism persisted as a separate entity. In many cases, Taoist priests preached the moral beliefs of the three religions to the masses, while passing on Taoist techniques of inner development to people secretly initiated into the Taoist way.

The Taiping Rebellion

Christian missionaries had been in China since early in the sixteenth century. By the mid-nineteenth century, the increase in trade between China and Europe and Britain encouraged more Christian missionaries to establish themselves in China, and Christianity spread among the common people. In keeping with the Chinese tradition of accepting more than one truth, Christian ideals became mixed with the existing religions of China.

A young man named Hong Xiu Zhuan (Hung Hsiueh Chuan), who had received Confucian training but repeatedly failed his civil service examination, announced that he was the younger brother of Jesus, appointed by God to wipe out the Manchu dynasty. Echoing Zhang Zhue's words seventeen hundred years earlier, Hong called his movement *Taiping,* or "Great

Peace," and like Zhang Zhue, he promised to bring a new heaven to earth, with himself as the Messiah.

The Taiping movement drew its followers from among the Chinese peasants and was a mixture of Christianity, Chinese folk tradition, and Confucianism. From 1850 to 1856, Hong waged war on the Chinese countryside, capturing city after city. His rebellion was finally put down by a combination of Manchu and Western forces. Although in some ways it resembled Taoist rebellions of earlier centuries, the Taiping movement was not Taoist. Indeed, one of the first groups singled out by the Taiping rebels for persecution was the Taoist priesthood. Many were executed.

Taoism in the Modern Age

Eventually, the increasing presence of Westerners led to antiforeign sentiment among the native Chinese. An uprising in 1900 against all Westerners was put down by an international force of European, American, and Japanese troops. The Manchu government, already weakened, found itself under still greater foreign influence. In 1911, it fell to yet another rebellion, and the long rule of the great Chinese dynasties was at an end.

The establishment of the Chinese Republic in 1912 was followed by decades of conflict—both civil war and war with Japan. Eventually this became a struggle between Communist and Nationalist forces within China. The two sides joined briefly to fight the Japanese in World War II, but after the war the internal struggle began again. In 1949, China fell to communism, and all religion was outlawed. The Nationalist Chinese fled to Taiwan, an island off the coast of mainland China, where they set up a competing government. One of the refugees was the sixty-third celestial master of the Taoist faith, the spiritual descendant of Zhang Dao Ling.

At the great Taoist centers on the mainland—places like Dragon-Tiger Mountain where the celestial masters had established their center, and Mount Mao, where the Highest Purity sect was founded—the practice of Taoism was officially forbidden but never quite stamped out. As it had so many times before, it lived on in the minds and hearts of the Chinese people.

CHAPTER 4

The Scriptures
and Beliefs
of Taoism

*T*he earliest writings on Taoism can be traced to the fourth century B.C.E. As Taoist sects arose, such as the Way of the Celestial Masters and the Highest Purity movement, their followers worked tirelessly to record their beliefs, liturgy, and rituals. Writings on Taoist themes continued steadily.

The approach of each sect differed greatly in detail and emphasis. Some sects, such as the Highest Purity Taoists of Mao Shan, stressed the importance of meditation as a means of finding Tao, while others concentrated on recording rituals and spells, alchemical formulas, and ways to gain immortality. But taken as a whole, the sects had a profound effect on Chinese thought. They extended Taoist philosophy beyond the imperial courts to workers and peasants, and they developed a complex system of beliefs that was distinct from both Chinese folk religions and other Chinese religious traditions.

The Taoist *Canon*

In the year 471 C.E., Taoist monks brought together the first *Tao Ts'ang (Daocang)*, or Taoist *Canon*. It drew from all of the main traditions of Taoism. The various sects recognized a common

basis in the *Tao Te Ching*, which, according to legend, stemmed from the five-thousand-character manuscript Laozi left behind as he was leaving Luoyang and the Zhou court. Its interpretation by later masters gave rise to much of the rest of the *Canon*, and it is the primary source for Taoist studies on the meaning of life. Since the second century of the common era, Taoists have considered the *Tao Te Ching* to be divinely revealed scripture.

The first Taoist *Canon* contained twelve hundred scrolls. Besides including the interpretations of the *Tao Te Ching*, the *Canon* included writings on alchemy and immortality, the lives of immortals and heroes, and good works and longevity. It had philosophical essays and folktales, magic words and meditation, ritual and liturgy, and many other aspects of Taoist thought.

In 748, the Tang emperor Tang Xuan-cong, who traced his ancestry to Laozi, sent scholars all over China to collect Taoist works. Not wishing to disappoint the emperor, the scholars reputedly returned with 7,300 scrolls. These scrolls became the second Taoist *Canon*.

In about 1016, with printing established in China, the *Canon* was revised under the direction of the Song dynasty. Some of the works collected under the Tangs were cast out, so that the third *Canon* contained only 4,565 scrolls. A final version was produced in 1444, during the Ming dynasty. This work of 5,318 scrolls is the largest body of scripture in the world.

Much of the *Tao Ts'ang* is incomprehensible today. The writing is full of cryptic symbols and references whose meanings have been lost over time. But the modern *Tao Ts'ang* is still the primary source of Taoist thought. It contains the philosophy that lies at the root of Taoist belief, as well as the tales and parables, rituals and practices, that have transmitted the Taoist religion down through the centuries.

Tao as the Ultimate Reality

The *Tao Te Ching* begins with a question: What is Tao? The writer answers:

> *The Tao that can be told*
> *is not the eternal Tao.*

The name that can be named
is not the eternal Name.

According to the writer, Tao is deeper than the deepest mystery the mind can imagine. It cannot be explained because it is too vast for human comprehension. Before anything existed, there was Tao. When nothing exists any longer, Tao will still be. No one can fully explain Tao because the limited human mind does not have the capacity to understand it.

Tao cannot be seen, touched, or otherwise experienced with the senses, but it is expressed by the natural forces of the universe. Like the universe, it is without beginning and without end. Zhuangzi, one of the great early Taoist masters, explains, "There is nowhere where it is not."

But at the same time, Tao is invisible and mysterious: what can be seen, heard, or felt is not truly Tao, which is above all things. The *Zhuangzi* says:

Tao has reality and evidence but no action and form.
It may be transmitted, yet not possessed.
It existed before Heaven and Earth and lasts forever. . . .

Tao is the beginning of all things. According to the *Tao Te Ching*:

The Tao gives birth to one,
One gives birth to two,
Two give birth to three,
Three give birth to all things.

Taoists understand this to mean that the vast, formless Tao existed before anything else. From it came the origin of being, or One. From this One came the balance of opposing forces, yin and yang, which are opposite but inseparable. Yin and yang are expressed in the three forces of the universe: heaven, earth, and humanity. From these three come everything else. Thus, Tao is the ultimate force or the reality behind everything.

Taoists accept that they can never fully understand Tao. What they focus on is finding a way to get into harmony with this ultimate force—to "go with the flow" of Tao and the universe.

■ **Finding Harmony in the Universe**
Outwardly go along with the flow, while inwardly keeping your true nature. Then your eyes and ears will not be dazzled, your thoughts will not be confused, while the spirit within you will expand greatly to roam in the realm of absolute purity.
*—from the **Huainanzi***

■ Translating from the Chinese

The Chinese language has no tenses, no singulars and plurals, no articles, and makes no gender distinctions. A given character may be used as a noun or as a verb, or even both in the same sentence, and Chinese words have many shades of meaning. Readers of Chinese understand all of these meanings simultaneously. Translators can only try to capture the general idea of the original. Many translators feel that a free—that is, inexact—translation of Chinese is often closer to the intent of the original than a literal, or exact translation. Here, for comparison, are several translations of the first lines of Chapter 4 of the **Tao Te Ching.**

The Way is like an empty vessel
That yet may be drawn from
Without ever needing to be filled.
It is bottomless; the very progenitor of all things in the world.
—Arthur Waley

The Way is a void
Used but never filled
An abyss it is
Like an ancestor
From which all things come.
—R. B. Blakney

The Tao is empty [like a bowl]
It is used, though perhaps never full
It is fathomless, possibly the progenitor of all things.
—from **Sources of Chinese Tradition,** deBary

The Tao seems to be very hollow and transparent and empty, but when you use it, it's inexhaustible. It is very deep and mysterious. It's like the ancestor of all things.
—Al Huang

The Tao is like a well:
used but never used up.
It is like the eternal void:
Filled with infinite possibilities.
—Stephen Mitchell

All of these translations say the same thing, but not in the same way. All are "right"—that is, all are faithful to the general idea of the lines— yet all are different. The variations suggest why people have been reading and discussing the Tao Te Ching for centuries and why many people say that there is no translation that is as good as reading it in the original Chinese.

Not-Being

The Tao from which all being comes is called the Great Void—an emptiness or "not-being." The Taoist seeks union with this emptiness, which is seen as a higher state than consciousness or thought. Taoists cultivate wuwei, which is often described as non-doing. This has sometimes been interpreted as an invitation to withdraw from society, but it is actually a kind of higher action, one in harmony with the natural order.

Wisdom and serenity come from conforming one's life to the natural laws of the universe. The notion of not-being is often associated with Taoist meditation, which requires an emptying of the mind so that the creative forces of Tao can flow in.

Harmony and Balance: Yin and Yang

People cannot see Tao, but they can experience it in the rhythmic cycles of nature: night and day, winter and summer, rain and sun, death and birth. These opposing forces of the natural world express the Chinese concept of yin and yang. The specific notion of yin and yang was not originally Taoist, but it fit with what Laozi and the other early Taoists believed. By the time of the Huainan masters, it had been absorbed into Taoist belief. The Huainanzi developed the yin-yang concept and brought it into the *Canon*.

The concept of yin and yang is central to Taoist understanding. These two forces demonstrate Tao, and because Tao is in everything, yin and yang are a part of Tao. Yang is the heavenly force. It is the force of movement, of light, fire, warmth, and life. *Yang* literally means "the sunny side" of a hill. In Chinese, *sun* is *tai yang*, or "great yang."

Yin, the shady side of the hill, is yang's opposite, but it cannot be separated from yang. Just as there can be no shadow without sun, there can be no yin without yang. The two operate together, in the cycles that are a part of nature and of Tao. The *Huainanzi* explains:

> *Tao can be concise, but stretched quite long;*
> > *dark, but shine brightly; weak, but become strong.*
> *It is the axle of the four seasons.*

■ The inscription on this painting reads, "This is Laozi worshiped by iron-smiths." In his hands, Laozi holds the symbol of yin and yang surrounded by the symbols of the eight trigrams, broken and unbroken lines that represent aspects of Taoist thought.

爐鐵行人供之　此是老君爺手托八卦面放金

It contains Yin and Yang,
Binding together the universe. . . .
Long ago, in the very beginning,
   the two emperors [Yin and Yang]
   having attained the Tao's authority,
   were established in the center.
Their spirits then spread far and wide,
   ruling the four directions.
This is why the heavens move and the earth is stable.
Turning and evolving without exhaustion. . . .
Like a potter's wheel, revolving round,
   returning to the starting point.

The concept of yin and yang sums up all of the opposing forces in life. But as the Taoist sees it, these forces are not truly opposites. They complement each other, resolving their differences in the great circle that symbolizes the unity of Tao.

The Relative Unimportance of All Things

The opposing forces represented by yin and yang are not permanently fixed. Taoists see all things as relative to one another. A cloudy day is yin—dark—when compared to a sunny one. But it is yang—bright—when compared to night. If you were to ask a Taoist whether something were "good or bad," a Taoist might respond, "Compared to what?"

To a Taoist, good and bad, yes and no, are not very far apart, so it is possible to accept the troubles of life calmly. The way of nature is neither right nor wrong—it simply is. Taoists attempt to be like nature itself. In nature, everything is constantly changing from yang to yin and back again. In life, no one can tell how things may turn out. Indeed, if one waits long enough, what appears to be good fortune may turn out to be a disaster, and what seems to be bad luck may be good. Success and failure, wealth and poverty, fame and obscurity all have equal drawbacks. Thus, all things are really the same in Tao.

In Taoism, simply being, or getting along as nature does, comes ahead of achievement. Too much pride causes people to be brought low. Like water, Taoists take the low ground. Water in itself is soft and yielding, but it melts the hardest things. It lies in the low places of the earth, but it nourishes all life. This is the "valley spirit," which never dies. To a Taoist, creation is passive, yin, the "mysterious female" that gives birth to all. Taoists try to develop this stillness within themselves, through meditation and devotional activities that bring calm and peace. In trying to be like nature, they cultivate an appreciation for the natural world. Taoists are close to Tao in natural settings, on mountaintops and in peaceful valleys.

People and the Way of Nature

In Taoism, there is no rebirth into a heavenly kingdom after death as there is in Christianity. Nor is there reincarnation, or rebirth in another form, as there is in Buddhism. The Taoist focuses on life here and now, life in this world. As the twentieth-century writer Lin Yutang describes it, the Taoist is:

> . . . one who starts out with this earthly life as all
> we can or need to bother about, wishes to live intently
> and happily as long as his life lasts, often has a sense
> of poignant sadness about this life and faces it cheerily,
> has a keen appreciation of the beautiful and the good
> in human life wherever he finds them, and regards
> doing good as its own satisfactory reward.

Taoists hope to have a long earthly life, and they try to do everything possible to see that they will have such a life. Living according to Taoist principles requires self-discipline, self-awareness, and self-control.

Taoists resist the desires and excesses that threaten to rob them of life. They hope, through the practice of various life-enhancing activities such as exercise, meditation, and healthful diet, to live a very long time. They believe that by so doing, they will become xian, able to achieve immortality in the present life.

Taoists see human beings as a natural part of the universe. Therefore, the life of a person who brings his or her life into complete harmony with the natural laws and cycles of the universe should continue to exist as long as heaven and earth exist.

Stories about Taoist sages describe how they became xian, or immortal. In these stories, the sages died and were buried, but later their coffins were opened to reveal not a body but a bamboo cane or a sword. The Taoists understand these changes to mean that although the body appears to die, what has really died is the emblem to which the person has given his likeness. The person's true body has gone away and dwells in the paradise of the immortals.

A Taoist pursues immortality in the present life with the hope that by the time of death, he or she will have been transformed. Ideally, his or her real, immortal body will already be present within the shell of the mortal body that is visible to others. Taoists try to transform their bodies by nurturing the forces of yang, or life, within themselves.

■ *People practice taijiquan outside the walls of Beijing's Forbidden City.*

The Three Treasures

Taoism stresses the importance of preserving the "three treasures" of human life: vitality, energy, and spirit. These three elements are both inseparable and interdependent. One cannot exist without the other two. Vitality, or *jing (ching)*, is associated with creativity and with basic body functions, including procreation. Energy, or *qi (ch'i)*, the essence of life, is associated with movement and strength. Spirit, or *shen*, is associated with consciousness, intellect, and spirituality.

These three elements must be kept in harmony and balance. Qi is especially important because of its influence on the other two; therefore, Taoists have developed many practices aimed at controlling and preserving qi. One of these is taijiquan, the system of movement aimed at helping people to control their qi, the energy flow within their bodies. Many of the movements of taiji were developed from the movements of animals. In the grace and power of animals, early Taoist masters saw natural qi. The stylized movements of taiji help those who practice it to unite with that natural qi force. The names of the movements reveal their origins: swallow returning to nest, clutching eagle, crane standing on one leg, cat looking at the moon. The graceful, circular motions reflect the natural cycles that are Tao.

Taoists also cultivate aspects of shen, the center of all emotions, thoughts, and intentions. They understand that shen may be wasted through passions, distractions, excesses of qi or jing, and generally "going overboard."

The *Tao Te Ching* admonishes followers to be yielding and passive, because "the gentlest thing in the world overcomes the hardest," and counsels against being ambitious or competitive:

> *Fill your bowl to the brim*
> *and it will spill.*
> *Keep sharpening your knife*
> *and it will be blunt.*
> *Chase after money and security*
> *and your heart will never unclench.*
> *Care about people's approval and you will be their prisoner.*
> *Do your work, then step back.*
> *The only path to serenity.*

This "stepping back" from the stresses of life brings a peace of mind that is a way of coming into greater harmony with Tao.

> *When you realize where you come from,*
> *you naturally become tolerant,*
> *disinterested, amused,*
> *kindhearted as a grandmother,*
> *dignified as a king.*
> *Immersed in the wonder of the Tao,*
> *you can deal with whatever life brings you.*

Worldly ambitions drain the energies. Turning away from desire and ambition is the way to become one with Tao.

The Taoist Pantheon

Many lifelong Taoists are content to live with the understanding that they are a part of the universal reality that is Tao and that they will one day return to Tao when their earthly life ends. These Taoists strive to live according to Taoist philosophy, to maintain balance and calm. They work to bring their lives into harmony with Tao through meditation, diet, taijiquan, and similar devotional practices.

Other Taoists, however, believe that in the words of Laozi, "Every being in the universe is an expression of Tao." They identify the different forces of nature and being with individual spirits or gods. Their beliefs are sometimes called religious, or "popular" Taoism.

There is a pantheon—a great glittering array of gods—for the person who follows religious Taoism; everything in the universe, both seen and unseen, is controlled by a god. There are gods of heaven and gods of earth, gods of longevity and gods of immortality, gods of medicine and health, and gods of mercy and conflict. There are gods for cities and gods for nature—rivers and streams, rain and wind, grass and trees. There is a god for every flower and a Queen of All Flowers. There are gods of the stars, Sire Thunder and Mother of Lightning, and powerful gods of the regions of earth—North, South, East, West, and Center.

There are gods for common, everyday things such as walls and ditches. One of the most popular of the gods is the Kitchen God, sometimes known as the God of Stoves, who oversees the home life of families and around whom one of the most common domestic rituals is celebrated.

In popular Taoist belief, each mountain and river is ruled by a particular god. Some of these gods were once human, such as Zhang Dao Ling, the father of religious Taoism. His deified spirit now rules at Lung Hu Shan, Dragon-Tiger Mountain. The mountain gods are especially powerful, and it is to the mountains that Taoists go when they want to be close to Tao. Achieving harmony with the natural world implies a closeness to nature, and the mountains are particularly sacred to Taoists.

Another category of celestials, or heavenly beings, is that of heroes and ancestors. Even before Taoism emerged as a religion, the Chinese revered their ancestors as if they were gods. It is believed that ancestors can intercede with the gods to aid and protect their living descendants. Similarly, Chinese heroes are also worshiped as gods. These heroic figures need not have been Taoists to be included in the Taoist pantheon—some Taoist gods were Confucians or Buddhists. They have become shen, or godlike, by doing great deeds for society, dying in battle, or displaying outstanding virtue and goodness.

The Three Pure Ones

At the top, in the supreme, highest, prior heavens, reign the Three Pure Ones, the gods of heaven, earth, and human beings. The Three Pure Ones figure prominently in Taoist ritual. They are aspects of Tao that appear as "heavenly worthies" or celestial beings. The Three Pure Ones may be identified as Heavenly Worthy of Primordial Being, who represents the beginning of all existence; Heavenly Worthy of Numinous Treasure, who represents the mysterious and nameless Tao; and Heavenly Worthy of the Way and Its Power. In some traditions, the latter two Pure Ones may be personified as Laozi and either Huang Di, the Yellow Emperor, or Ling Pao, the Jade Emperor. But their specific identities are not important. Together, they are the spirit and mystery of Tao and the highest goals of humanity.

The Jade Emperor's Court

Beneath the prior heavens are the posterior heavens, a little lower, yet still exalted. These heavens are ruled by the Jade Emperor and are crowded with lesser gods and immortals.

These heavens are organized much like the imperial court of ancient China. The Jade Emperor, Ling Pao, personally directs and manages all of the affairs of heaven and earth. It is important to note, however, that the Jade Emperor is not like the all-powerful one God of Judaism, Christianity, and Islam. He does not always get his way. The forces of yin and yang are at work even in the Taoist heaven, and heavenly life is a continuing struggle against the forces of evil that the Jade Emperor's forces sometimes lose.

The Immortals

Among the Taoist gods is a group called the Eight Immortals. As immortals, the eight can fly through the air, appear and disappear at will, and use their magic to help people in need. They are called on for such diverse matters as minor illnesses, bothersome evil spirits, desire for male offspring, money troubles, and hope for longevity.

> ### ■ The Ba Xian (Eight Immortals)
>
> **Lu Dongbin,** also known as Lu Yan, is the historical figure on whose writings Quanzhen Taoism is based. Associated with medicine, he also has charms to tame evil spirits. His emblem is a sword.
>
> **Di Kuai Li** is associated with medicine. Bad-tempered and eccentric, he appears as a beggar. His symbol is the crutch, and he fights for the poor and the weak.
>
> **Zhang Kuo Lau,** a great magician, carries a musical instrument. He is often consulted by families who are desiring male offspring.
>
> **Cao Kuo Qin,** known as a stern judge, carries an imperial tablet of recommendation.
>
> **Han Xiang Zi** is a great poet and musician and the patron of musicians. His symbol is a jade flute.
>
> **Han Zhung Li,** formerly a Han general, is associated with immortality. He carries a feathery fan that calms angry seas.
>
> **Lan Cai Ho,** although touched by insanity, is favored by the gods. He may appear as either a man or a woman. He carries a magic flower basket.
>
> **Ho Xian Ku** is the only woman among the Eight Immortals. She carries a lotus flower.

Images of the Eight Immortals can be found almost everywhere in the world in which Chinese people work and live: in shrines or Taoist temples; painted on wall scrolls, fans, vases, and teapots; carved into wood, porcelain, and earthenware; or cast in bronze. Of these immortals, some are more powerful than others and can act alone. Some can act only in cooperation with others. Each immortal has a symbol with which he or she is able to work magic.

Some of the Eight Immortals were historical figures, dating to around the time of the Tang dynasty or earlier. The most powerful of the eight, and also the most popular, is Lu Dongbin (Lu Tong Pin). The immortal Lu Dongbin is none other than Ancestor Lu, or Lu Yan, the forerunner of the Complete Reality Taoists and the author of the Hundred Character Tablet in the *Tao Ts'ang*. A major figure in the history and philosophy of Taoism, he is associated in popular belief with medicine and eternal life. He also has

■ *Lu Dongbin, a Taoist scholar and the author of the* **Hundred Character Tablet,** *was the forerunner of Complete Reality Taoism. One of the Eight Immortals, he is always depicted with a sword.*

power over evil spirits, and he carries a sword with which he can tame demons if he is properly approached.

Han Zhung Li, another of the Eight Immortals, was a Han dynasty general who converted to Taoism. Others, like Zhang Kuo Lau and Ho Xian Ku, were common folk who had attracted the attention of the gods through suffering unjust treatment without complaint and giving to others without thought for themselves. Tested by the gods and found worthy, they became immortal.

Personal Gods

In contrast to the gods whose origins lie entirely in natural phenomena, such as the gods of earth and water, are the many personal gods. These were once people who did great deeds during their lifetimes and whose spirits, therefore, continue to exist. Over time, they have been elevated to the status of gods by the declarations of religious leaders or emperors. They are often associated with particular areas of influence, and Taoists pray to them, requesting their help. Believers try to emulate the examples each of these personal gods set while living.

Such gods as She, God of Land, and Hou Ji, God of Agriculture, were legendary officials under the rule of the Yellow Emperor. Other gods, like the gods of rain and fire, can also be traced to legendary or historical figures.

War heroes might also become personal gods. Kuan Yu, or Kuan Jung, was a famous general during the period of the Three Kingdoms in the early part of the third century C.E. Refusing to surrender in battle, he was captured and executed by the enemy. Each succeeding generation glorified his memory until one of the Tang emperors declared him a god. Because he was also known for keeping meticulous financial records, he has become the patron of bookkeepers. A popular god in many temples, he is often depicted as standing nine feet tall with red cheeks, a magnificent black beard, and bushy eyebrows.

Another personal god is Sheng Mu, who was named Heavenly Empress during the Qing dynasty. The daughter of a fisherman, she helped the farmers, fishers, and their families in her village by casting out demons before she died at the young age of

■ Magu is a female immortal associated with the Queen of the Western Heavens. It is said that during Magu's long earthly life, the Eastern Sea dried up three times, thus allowing people to walk from the mainland to the magical island of Penglai, the home of immortal beings who possessed the secrets of eternal life.

twenty-one. Now patron of fishers and farmers, she keeps with her two of the demons that she tamed. They act as messengers, bringing the needs of the people to her attention so that she can rush to their aid.

The Demon World

The gods of the Taoists are challenged by demons, or Kuei, that plague the natural and human worlds. These demons may be natural forces, such as typhoons, epidemics, fires, and droughts. They may also be men or women who have died violent, meaningless deaths. Sometimes they are "orphan souls," people who have no families to remember them or who have been improperly buried and have no ancestor tablet to keep their memory alive.

These unhappy demons roam the world and cause sickness and other hardships. In their efforts to be remembered, they use the forces of nature to draw attention to themselves. Taoists do not worship demons, but they do believe they exist. Thus, they try to bargain with them and placate them, often by asking a god or an immortal to intercede. The continuous struggle between gods and demons is part of the popular interpretation of yin and yang, the balance of opposing forces that is Tao.

CHAPTER 5

Ritual and Meditation

Ritual, the formal acts that make up religious observance, has been an important feature of Taoist worship since the time of Zhang Dao Ling in the second century of the common era. Today, priests trained in ritual words and actions, meditation, and scripture lead intricate forms of worship and praise handed down through sixty-four generations of celestial masters. These rituals express the continuing renewal of the universe and remind people of the harmony of Tao, the balance of yin and yang, the interaction of heaven, earth, and humanity, and the constant struggle between order and chaos.

Taoist ritual is a feast for the senses. Colorful robes, banners, statues and paintings of gods and immortals, instrumental music and song, chanting, liturgy, dance, incense, candles, lamplight, and even firecrackers work together to create an experience rich with meaning for participants and observers.

Through their religious observances, Taoists participate in keeping their world orderly and harmonious by celebrating the ultimate reality of Tao. The rituals they practice promote the well-being of their families, their ancestors, and their community, and keep evil away.

The Jiao

The basic Taoist ritual held to enhance the welfare of living people is the jiao. *Jiao* means "offering," so a jiao may be a simple ritual offering of wine and food at a family altar. However, it is often a far more elaborate celebration. A jiao may be performed as part of the regular observance of the Taoist calendar or for a special occasion such as the consecration of a new temple. A jiao of this type is not a single ritual but an entire ritual program, a series of individual rites conducted for different purposes, such as summoning the gods, blessing the land, or redeeming lost souls. The ritual celebration may last for three days.

The priests, who often travel some distance to participate, select the rituals for the occasion. These vary with the length and purpose of the jiao. Any of these individual rituals may be conducted separately or in combination with others at other times during the year.

A major jiao celebration often includes a community festival. While the priests and other participants are performing rituals inside the temple, the festival is going on outside. Only the priests, their attendants, and community leaders observe the sacred rites. Other members of the community celebrate the jiao by attending the festival and enjoying the colorful pageantry when the priests come outside. Festivals feature such entertainment as theatrical presentations on Taoist themes and martial arts demonstrations. Food stands are many, and vendors sell religious items such as paper ghost money, which is burned in offerings. There is a brisk trade in firecrackers, which Taoists use to scare away any yin spirits that might be lurking nearby. Large papier-mâché figures, made for the occasion, serve as "guardians" of the festival and keep an eye on the proceedings. Both the festival in the streets and the ritual within the temple may go on for several days.

For three days before the jiao, the priests live in the temple, preparing themselves. The night before the jiao begins, the priests perform a purification ritual. Oil is heated to the boiling point in a wok, or bowl-shaped metal container. While the priests chant prayers and use a buffalo horn to summon the heavenly visitors, a "redhead," a priest wearing a red headdress, throws alcohol on

the oil, causing flames to shoot heavenward. Everything that will be used in the jiao—robes, scrolls, musical instruments, incense sticks, candles—is passed over the flames and made ready.

The first day of the jiao begins with a procession of priests, acolytes, cantors, musicians, and the keeper of incense. The priests then call on the Three Pure Ones—the gods of heaven, earth, and humanity—to be present at the ritual. The high priest lights incense in each of the five directions of the universe and offers a general confession. In a second procession, the priests offer incense to the gods.

Outside the temple, the priests raise a long, rectangular, yellow banner to attract the gods' attention. The red inscription on the banner invites the gods to enter the temple and asks for their protection and help.

The morning rituals are followed by a noon offering. Each priest performs a song and a dance, thus displaying his talents to the gods. Each priest then ceremoniously places a gift such as a flower, tea, a candle, or fruit, on the altar. The noon offering is repeated every day of the jiao.

Afternoon ceremonies may include the Division of the Lamps, a ritual that symbolizes the coming of light to the world. With the temple in total darkness, fire is brought in to the temple, and candles are lighted one at a time and placed before each of the Three Pure Ones, accompanied by the singing of hymns. The ritual represents these lines from the *Tao Te Ching:*

Tao gives birth to one,
One gives birth to two,
Two give birth to three,
Three give birth to all things.

These lines also form the basis of the ritual for the Return to Unity, in which the separate lights representing "all things" are combined into one and finally embodied in the priest, who at that moment becomes one with the great void, or Tao.

Throughout the day, the priests perform other rituals. The consecration of a new temple, for example, may include rites to prevent fire and to enrich the soil and bring prosperity to the community. At day's end, the priests invite the immortals to come from the sacred mountains and join the celebration. Then all of the participants chant prayers to suppress yin, the negative force of the universe, and encourage yang, the positive force. The priests say the prayers for the night and then seal the altar.

The second day, like the first, is full of rituals, some calling on the gods to be present and others asking for the salvation of wandering souls or for the preservation of the community. Some rituals may be carried out at a distance from the temple, with the festival-goers joining the sacred procession.

On the third day, the priests read from the scriptures and make memorial offerings. The afternoon includes a special offering to the Three Pure Ones. Part of the offering ritual includes the hanging of a large, black banner from the ceiling of the temple. The banner represents the heavenly bridge that the divine guests will use to come to earth and then to return to their celestial home. As music plays, two of the celebrants sit, and all of the other participants kneel. The deities are invited once again, from the least to the most powerful. As the ritual proceeds, three kneeling priests sing sacred verses, while the seated priests wave banners over the backs of the community representatives to drive away evil. A firecracker explodes, and the music stops. This ritual is repeated six times. Then all of the participants stand and proceed to the altar, where incense and wine are offered to the Three Pure Ones. The banquet of the gods over, the altar is sealed once more, and the jiao is ended.

The Universal Salvation

Although it is not technically part of the jiao, or offering to the gods, a final ritual follows: the ritual of Universal Salvation. Its purpose is to comfort and appease the "homeless souls," the nameless dead who wander without having been given a proper burial. As the yellow banner outside the temple is taken down to be burned, the priests exit the temple, chanting. There they find a huge banquet awaiting them, a banquet of every imaginable kind of food: cakes, bread, fruit—even canned goods. Sticks of incense perfume the table.

The priests bless the food. After another procession, they display a writ, or document, to the lost souls, inviting them to the table. The high priest uses special finger movements borrowed from Buddhism, along with a bowl of sacred water, to transform himself into a Heavenly Worthy. With singing and chanting, he passes incense over the food. At last, he tosses the food he has blessed to the crowd.

Finally, the papier-mâché decorations and the special documents are burned in a huge bonfire. The festival is over.

Other Rituals

Less elaborate Taoist festivals occur throughout the year. On the fifteenth day of the seventh month (August), Taoists celebrate the birthday of the earth god. It is a time to help lost souls. The ritual associated with this festival is the Floating of the Water Lamps. After the proper invocations, three Taoist priests and their musicians lead a procession to a place where there is flowing water. One member of every Taoist household joins the march. The priests chant, and then the participants place lighted candles in small paper lanterns or boats and float them on the stream. The candles guide the liberated souls on their journey upward.

If a Universal Salvation ritual is to be held also, the ghosts of the drowned are invited to the feast. Otherwise food may be

spread for the drowned souls who have been left unburied in watery graves. This festival has deep significance for the people of a country where the Yangtze River overflowed its banks regularly each year, carrying off as many as one hundred thousand people at a time. It is celebrated by both Buddhists and Taoists, but even in the Buddhist celebration, Taoist priests perform the ritual part of the ceremony and summon the souls of the dead.

Taoist priests may also be called on to perform the ritual of exorcism—that is, the driving out of evil spirits—in a home or at an outdoor location. The priests use all of the trappings of Taoist ritual—flags, incense, water, swords, and peachwood whips—and move in a procession through the area where the offending spirits may be, chanting ritual words to drive them away. Other rites for driving out ghosts or monsters also make use of sword-play. On a festival day similar to Halloween, people wear masks and stage mock struggles between the evil spirits and the sword-wielding Taoists.

Domestic Rituals

Taoists are encouraged to practice their religion on their own, without the intervention of a priest. Many Taoist homes have altars or shrines that contain their ancestor tablet, a kind of family tree. At the home altar, both men and women conduct the rites for health and prosperity, for healing in times of sickness, or in memory of their ancestors. They may light incense and candles, burn offerings such as the paper ghost money that symbolizes family wealth, and chant words from the *Tao Ts'ang*.

Ancestor Rites

Ancestor rites are very important in Chinese culture, which places a high value on family and continuity. Families will often hold private memorials for their ancestors before celebrating a festival meal like the one served to welcome the new year. A simple ancestor memorial might include the burning of incense and a libation, or ritual pouring, of wine at the family altar, as well as prayers in which family members share the events of the day with their ancestor and ask the ancestor's blessing.

More elaborate ancestor rites require that the home altar be arranged in a special way, with incense in the middle and flowers and candles on either side. Foodstuffs, including meat, beans, fruit, soup, cookies, rice, tea, and wine, are offered to the ancestors in a prescribed order. A member of the family reads an

■ *A family refurbishes an ancestor's tomb and leaves fresh flowers as part of the annual Tomb Sweeping Festival in the spring.*

official ritual document modeled on forms in the *Tao Ts'ang*. At this time, the family may open the ancestor tablet and add the names of anyone who has recently died.

In early April, families celebrate a festival in which they refurbish the tombs of their ancestors. They burn incense and offer wine to the ancestor spirits, and make small fires in which they burn paper ghost money and other offerings. For those who have recently lost loved ones, it is a time to mourn; but it is also a time to celebrate family togetherness with visits and, as is customary in all Taoist celebrations, a shared banquet.

■ The Chinese Calendar

The Chinese reckoning of time begins in the year 2637 B.C.E. In that year, according to legend, the prime minister of the court of Huang Di, the Yellow Emperor, worked out the cycle of sixty years that is the center of the Chinese calendar. This Sexagenary Cycle is very important, both in predicting the future and in recording age. A Chinese person's most important birthday is the sixtieth, when he or she has completed one Sexagenary Cycle.

The Sexagenary Cycle is based on the Five Elements: metal, wood, fire, earth, and water. Each element has two sides, yin and yang. These ten sides are called the Heavenly Stems. Each stem is also associated with a color. The yang side of wood, for example, is green, and the yin side, blue.

The ten Heavenly Stems combine with twelve Earthly Branches. Each Earthly Branch is represented by an animal: monkey, rooster, dog, pig, rat, ox, tiger, rabbit, dragon, snake, horse, and goat. Thus, a Chinese year is described as The Year of the Silver Goat or The Year of the Purple Monkey. It takes sixty years for an animal and a color to match again and for the cycle to be repeated.

In the Taoist religion, six gods are associated with each of the Heavenly Stems. The Six Gods of Chia (Male, Wood) and the Six Gods of Ting (Female, Fire), especially, hold magic powers that help these gods subdue dragons, move mountains, and perform similar miracles.

The Taoist Year

All of the Taoist ritual celebrations are part of a regular calendar of Taoist festivals. Most festivals mark the birthday of a

god or other heavenly worthy. Many important celebrations fall on or around the fifteenth of the month.

The festival year begins with New Year's Day—the first day of the first month of the Chinese calendar. In general, the first Chinese month corresponds to February on the Western calendar. On New Year's Day, Taoists celebrate the rebirth of yang, the positive force of the universe, into the world. Rituals in the Taoist temples and in the homes welcome the Three Pure Ones of the Highest Heavens with an offering of sweets, or tien (in Chinese, *tien* means both "heaven" and "sweet"). Wooden blocks, cast like dice, determine when the gods have finished their banquet. When the blocks turn up together three times in a row, the gods are considered to have finished their meal and to have said yes to the

■ *On New Year's Eve, older family members give children red envelopes containing money, representing hopes for prosperity in the coming year.*

People in Chinatowns around the world celebrate the New Year with a dragon dance honoring the rebirth of yang, the positive force of the universe, into the world.

hopes and prayers that have been expressed. At home, an ancestor offering is made, and the family celebrates the coming of a new year with a banquet, gifts, the exchange of good wishes, and visits to friends and relatives.

The religious calendar is divided into three parts: the Reign of the Spirits of Heaven, the Reign of the Forgiver of Sins, and the Reign of the Water Spirits. The Reign of the Spirits of Heaven is the longest. It begins on the fifteenth day of the new year and lasts for six months. A banquet is served to the gods in the temple and then taken home to be eaten by the family. Children carry toy lanterns through the streets to guide the heavenly spirits on their way. On the first day of the New Year festival, which lasts for a week, a dragon dance winds through the streets. The dragon follows a child carrying a bright red ball, which is the symbol of yang hidden in a dark sea of yin. The dragon swallows the ball to bring long life, immortality, and union with the heavenly spirits. Strings of firecrackers are lighted to frighten away yin spirits.

As the Reign of the Spirits of Heaven draws to a close, the gates of hell are opened. The lost souls of unjust people, evil doers, and others who have wandered from Tao get a second chance. The living can liberate these lost souls by performing good works during this time, such as giving to the poor.

On the fifteenth day of the seventh month, Taoists celebrate the birthday of the earth god, Zhung Yuan, with the Festival of the Earth Spirits. The celebrants perform the ritual of the Floating of the Water Lamps to guide the souls liberated during the opening of the gates of hell on their return journeys. This one-day festival ushers in the three-month Reign of the Forgiver of Sins.

The fifteenth day of the tenth month is the birthday of the God of Water. On this day, the Reign of the Water Spirits begins. Taoists celebrate the occasion with a banquet for the release of souls from the watery regions of the underworld. The water spirits' reign lasts until just before the New Year.

At the end of the Taoist year, in one of the most widely practiced domestic rituals, the kitchen god, who has been installed in every home to observe the doings of the family, is dispatched to heaven to report to the Jade Emperor. The kitchen god usually hangs on the kitchen wall, represented by a piece of paper that is burned to send it on its way to heaven. Soon after the coming of the New Year, the kitchen god is welcomed back, and the cycle begins again.

The Taoist calendar provides structure, but Taoists do not hold regularly scheduled worship services in the Western sense. Taoist temples and shrines are always open, and someone may drop in to light incense or perhaps to pray to the gods and then draw a slip from a bamboo tube. The slip holds a prediction for the future and refers the petitioner to a book of divination. Taoist

■ Calendar of Taoist Festivals

February (First Month)

1   New Year's Day, the Feast of the Three Pure Ones, the gods of heaven, earth, and man, who live in the prior (highest) heavens and from whom all visible things come

4   Seeing Off the Heavenly Spirits; Welcoming Back the Kitchen God

6   Birthday of the Jade Emperor, ruling god of the posterior (lower) heavens

15   Festival of the Spirits of Heaven
     Beginning of the first period of the religious year, the Reign of the Spirits of Heaven

March (Second Month)

2   Birthday of the Lord of the Soil. This servant of the Yellow Emperor caused crops to flourish.

16   Birthday of Laozi

19   Birthday of Kuan Shi Yin, female god of Taoism and Buddhism

April (Third Month)

23   Birthday of Sheng Mu, Empress of the Heavens

26   Birthday of Zhang Dao Ling, founder of religious Taoism

May (Fourth Month)

4   Birthday of Buddha

14   Birthday of Lu Dongbin, or Ancestor Lu, one of the Eight Immortals

June (Fifth Month)

5   Festival of the Summer Solstice. On this day, yang is at the height of its power.

July (Sixth Month)

28   Birthday of the God of Thunder

August (Seventh Month)

7–13 Opening of the gates of hell. During this time, release of lost souls can be won by offerings to the poor and with good works.

15   Festival of the Earth Spirits
     Birthday of the God of Earth
     Beginning of the second period of the religious year, the Reign of the Forgiver of Sins

September (Eighth Month)

15   Festival of the Autumn Moon

October (Ninth Month)

28   Birthday of Confucius

November (Tenth Month)

10   Festival of Yu the Great, patron spirit of community renewal

15   Birthday of the God of Water
     Beginning of the third period of the religious year, the Reign of the Water Spirits

December (Eleventh Month)

15   Winter Solstice and Solar New Year

January (Twelfth Month)

23–24 Return of the Kitchen God to heaven

seers then interpret the message. Someone with a particularly urgent problem may consult a priest, who will perform a special temple ritual. But it is not necessary to visit a temple at all in order to be a practicing Taoist. Many small roadside shrines commemorate places where something important occurred—a place where someone was saved from falling off a cliff, for example, or where someone escaped harm in an accident. Leaving offerings at these places is a form of Taoist worship.

Taoist Rites of Passage

As do most religious traditions, Taoism recognizes major events in life such as birth, death, and marriage. However, there is little in Taoist practice that corresponds directly to rites of passage, such as circumcision and bar and bat mitzvah in the Jewish tradition or baptism and confirmation in the Christian church. Rather, changes in a person's life status are marked with celebrations that reinforce the individual's place in the Taoist community, the family, and the natural universe.

Birth and Infancy

Children are much honored in Chinese life as symbols of family continuity and strength. Even before birth, Taoists believe a child is protected by Tai Shen, the guardian spirit of unborn children. A woman who is expecting a child will make suitable offerings to ensure a safe delivery and a healthy baby. Priests, too, may be asked to perform special rituals. After the baby's birth, the new mother once again makes offerings at shrines or temples. Articles of baby clothing are customary gifts to the female spirits who are themselves mothers and who look after women. A Taoist adult may be chosen to be a kind of godparent, someone who will help to keep the child safe and peaceful. Taoist charms may be used to predict what problems, if any, may beset the child, and to protect it from harm. When the baby is four months old, thanksgiving offerings of peach cakes are made in celebration of its health and safety. Friends and relatives bring sets of baby clothes, called head-to-foot presents, and more peach cakes, which are first placed on the altar and then passed around to the family's other children.

On the baby's first birthday, its parents celebrate its safe passage through the first year of life with a banquet for the neighborhood. The baby is offered a tray with items symbolizing different paths in life—hard work, intelligence, wealth, health, and scholarship, for example—and given its first bite of solid food. Finally, the baby gets a sweet rice cake to turn its thoughts from worldly to heavenly things.

Growing children are protected by a mother spirit, or *chuang mu*. A special offering of cooked rice is made to this spirit if the child is ill or fussy.

Children attend Taoist schools where they learn the fundamentals of Taoism. Small children chant and sing the words of the *Tao Te Ching*, committing them to memory as they enjoy their rhythms and sounds. As they grow older, both boys and girls learn meditations and Taoist hymns. They learn to play musical instruments that are used in private and public Taoist rituals. They are invited to participate in ceremonies for healing the sick, warding off evil, and offering sacrifices to gods, demons, and ancestors.

Young people also learn such practices as taijiquan and calligraphy, which have practical uses for their own sake but which have their roots in Taoist devotional practice.

There are no specific Taoist puberty rites. A jiao may be made at the family altar to celebrate a young person's completing his or her studies and becoming an adult.

Taoist Weddings

A wedding establishes the family, the center of Chinese life. The full wedding rite comes from the time of the Han dynasty (around 200 B.C.E.) and is rarely performed today. Full wedding ritual requires a formal exchange of birth dates, which are examined by a Taoist specialist. If the combination of birth dates makes an uneven, or yang, number, the announcement of the wedding is presented before the family altar with an offering of incense. The bride and groom exchange traditional gifts to seal the formal engagement, and a date is set for the wedding. The families may consult Taoist priests or fortunetellers on questions of proper ritual and for favorable dates.

On the day of the wedding, the bride and her parents visit the shrine of their ancestors. At the shrine, the parents recite these words, inserting the necessary names:

Our beloved daughter, sister of [brothers' names]
will this day be taken to her new home as a bride.
We solemnly announce these rites to our ancestors.

The bride's hair is arranged, and she is dressed in her wedding clothes. A ritual follows in which the bride is given a wine cup. She bows four times, showing respect for the four seasons and the four stages of life. She is instructed by the wedding celebrant to be a good wife to her husband, a good daughter-in-law, and a good mother. She does not answer, but assents silently. Her parents repeat the admonitions, and again she remains silent. Then her face is veiled, and she awaits the groom.

Following a ritual at the groom's ancestor shrine, in which the groom is reminded of his duties to the bride, a procession leads him to the bride's home. The ceremony itself is simple and takes place as part of a banquet. When everyone is assembled, the bride's veil is lifted, revealing her face. Everyone is asked to sit down, and the bride and groom drink from the wedding cup. They then sign a document of marriage, and the banquet proceeds.

The next day, the bride traditionally goes to the home of her husband's parents. She carries with her gifts that symbolize her intent to bear children for the family, and she worships at her husband's ancestor tablet.

Three days after the wedding, the bride visits her own parents. Her visit signifies that she is now a member of another family and that she is a visitor in her former home.

Taoist Funerals

Taoists believe that at death, the shen, or spirit, separates from the body, but remains nearby until the body is buried. Then that part of the spirit that governs passions, grief, and other strong feelings is buried with the body. The pure spiritual essence of the person survives, and goes on, either to peaceful rest or to face punishment from the gods for misdeeds on earth.

■ *Taoists believe that the actions of the living can help the spirits of the dead rest peacefully. Here, following an exorcism rite performed by a Taoist priest, a woman burns paper ghost money, clothes, and other familiar items as offerings to make the life of her dead child in the spirit world a happy one.*

The good works of the living and proper ritual can buy the dead person a reprieve from divine punishment. Funerals, therefore, are as lavish as a family can afford. Correct observance of Taoist funeral rites is so important to Taoists that an entire branch of the priesthood oversees it. Today, these are the "blackhead" Taoists, so-called for their black headdresses. The service for the dead can last from one to three days and includes Taoist music, ritual, and chants.

Elaborate rules regulate the care of the dying person, the actions of the care-givers at the time of death, and preparation of the body for the funeral. A Taoist priest is often summoned to oversee the preparations in the home and make sure that they are ritually correct.

The family altar and its decorations are covered with a white cloth, the color of yin, or sadness. The body is placed in the coffin, and the children of the family are invited to put the deceased's favorite things in with it. Children perform this service because they do not know the monetary value of things and will therefore choose truly, without thought of cost. The family prepares a banquet and puts the dead person's favorite foods in the coffin, as well as special charms or prayers written on slips of white paper. While the priest chants the ritual for the dead, the slips of paper are taken from the coffin and burned as offerings to send them to heaven, and new charms are added. When the ritual is complete, the coffin is sealed, and a banquet follows.

The burial day is determined by a Taoist calendar specialist, who chooses a favorable day for the event. On that day, a procession of priests, musicians, and mourners makes its way to the cemetery. The Taoist priests walk in front of the coffin, shaking bells, playing their instruments, and saying magic spells. These activities help to guide the dead person's spirit to its rest. So, from birth to death, Taoist rituals and festivals shape the lives of Taoist believers and work to keep them in harmony with the rhythms of the universe.

Meditation

The center of priestly life and of all Taoist practice is meditation. Meditation has a long history in religion, not only in Taoism, but in Buddhism and Islam as well.

The basis for Taoist meditation can be found in the *Tao Te Ching*, in which Chapter 16 begins, "Empty your mind of all thoughts." Early Taoist masters took up the recommendation of

Laozi and commented on it. The *Zhuangzi* records the words of a master named Yen Hui, who said this about meditation: "My connection with my body and all its parts is dissolved. Seeing and hearing are discarded. Thus leaving my material form, and quitting all my knowledge, I become one with the Great Void. This I call sitting and forgetting."

It has been said that someone can learn meditation in a day but must practice it for a lifetime in order to understand it fully. There are various levels of Taoist meditation. Only the most adept students ever reach the highest plane, in which they are united with Tao. At its simplest levels, students learn to empty their minds of all desires and emotions, all thoughts and wishes, and to channel spiritual energy within the body.

One of the things that students of meditation practice is breath control. In Taoist understanding, breathing does not simply mean the passage of air into and out of the lungs. In Taoist interpretation, breathing includes the way oxygen is carried to parts of the body in the bloodstream by the circulatory system and waste products are carried away. Taoists try to harness the energy of the breath, or qi, and guide it through the body by concentration. Eventually, they become adept at directing oxygen to places that might be hurting so that they can be healed. As Taoists advance in technique, they turn this process, too, over to the unconscious. They can then let the energizing qi go where it wants to go.

Taijiquan, an early Taoist system of exercises, developed as an aid to learning meditation, helps people channel qi around their bodies before they are able to do it with concentration alone. The goal of the exercises in concentration and meditation is to achieve "embryonic breathing." This is described as the way energy is transmitted effortlessly to the body of an unborn child. The whole process is one of physical and spiritual development, or "inner alchemy." At its end, the Taoist's vitality, energy, and spirit become one with Tao.

Another form of meditation requires students to visualize the gods of true life. This allows the gods to enter into a person and brings their blessings of life into the body. By visualizing the sun, the moon, the planets, the stars, and the heavenly gods, an individual can crowd out the demons of anger, suspicion, envy, and annoyance that wear down energy. Visualizing the gods brings people back to their natural state. It allows the gods to enter and set up their own presence within.

Learning Taoist meditation can take many years—even a lifetime. Students must give up all motivation and desire, even the desire to learn how to meditate or to have meditation "work." They must renounce all sense of individual identity and become totally absorbed in meditating for its own sake. In so doing, they become one with Tao, like water that is poured into water. Entering into the rhythms of nature, they find within themselves the inner light that is Tao.

CHAPTER 6

The Tao of the Arts

In the story told by Zhuangzi in Chapter 2, the master carver made an almost perfect bell stand. But before he could make it, he had to forget himself and all he had to gain. He had to let Tao take over. Once he came into harmony with the nature of the tree, the beautiful bell stand emerged from the wood without effort on his part.

Zhuangzi's story illustrates how the creative force of Tao can work in people who let it come into their minds and bodies. The idea of finding a "way"—Tao—to produce great art effortlessly, like the master carver, has always interested creative people. Taoism appealed to Chinese painters and poets, dancers and musicians. Eventually there came to be a Taoist "way" of doing these things. It became part of many Chinese art forms.

Tao and Literature

The early Taoists produced many forms of writing besides scripture and commentaries on Taoist philosophy. Essays, stories, parables, and satire appear in early Taoist manuscripts. Many Chinese folktales, fairy tales, fables, and romances from ancient

times contain elements of magic and mystery that can be linked to Taoism. During the Tang dynasty, all forms of art flourished, including literature. Writers told stories of time travel, ghostly worlds, and distant magical kingdoms, all showing a clear expression of the creative, magical side of Taoism.

Poetry, however, was the literary form that Taoism influenced most strongly. The *Tao Te Ching,* the foundation of Taoist scripture and thought, is a long poem. The *Tao Te Ching* and other poems of the early Taoist sages were admired and imitated from ancient times.

Between the third and the seventh centuries of the common era, Taoist and Buddhist beliefs about nature inspired new ways of treating nature in poetry. Reverence for nature became a major theme, along with human relationships and a longing for the past.

The poet Dao Qian (T'ao Ch'ien) (372–427 C.E.) was considered the finest poet of his time. A Confucian official, he became drawn to Taoism. Eventually he left his job with the court to live in and write about the world of nature. Many of his poems express the joys he felt of becoming one with nature, which is a Taoist ideal. Here Dao Qian expresses how that can be done, even in the city:

> *I have built my hut beside a busy road*
> *But I can hear no clatter from passing carts and horses.*
> *Do you want to know how?*
> *When the mind is detached, where you are is remote also.*
> *Picking chrysanthemums by the east hedge*
> *I can see the hills to the south a long way away:*
> *It is sunset and the air over the mountains is beautiful;*
> *Birds are flying in flocks back to their nests.*
> *This tastes real.*
> *I would like to talk about it, but there are no words.*

Poetry, like other art forms, flowered under the rule of the Tang emperors. This period became known as China's golden age of poetry. Many poems from this time are celebrations of nature. Often they suggest that natural wonders are hints of the divine world.

> ### ■ Non–Doing
>
> *According to Taoist philosophers, the Tao does nothing, yet there is nothing it does not do. Zhuangzi's conversation with his friend Huizi illustrates this concept. He uses uselessness as an image to show how people fail to understand the infinite, unending Tao:*
>
> *Huizi said to Zhuangzi, "I have a large tree. Its trunk is so gnarled and bent that no carpenter can find a use for it. Your words are like that tree. Large but useless, and not wanted by anyone."*
>
> *Zhuangzi responded, "Have you not seen a wild cat or a weasel? It lies crouching down, waiting for its prey. It leaps this way and that, high and low, but then gets caught in a trap and dies. A yak, on the other hand, is enormous, but it cannot catch a rat. Now you have a large tree and are worried about its usefulness. Why don't you plant it in the realm of Nothingness, so you may wander by its side in inaction and lie under it in repose? The reason it does not fall to the ax is that it cannot be exploited. Being of no use—why should that be a problem?"*

One of the best-known poets of the age was a Taoist named Li Bai (Li Po) (701–762). Li Bai wrote more than one thousand poems. Many of them center on the natural life of the Taoist. In "On the Mountain," he explains a hermit's reasons for living in the wilderness:

> *You ask me:*
>   *Why do I live*
> *on this green mountain?*
>   *I smile*
>   *No answer*
>   *My heart serene*
> *On flowing water*
>   *peachblow*
>   *quietly going*
>   *far away*
>   *another earth*
> *This is*
>   *another sky*
> *No likeness*
>   *to that human world below*

Life during the Tang period was far from serene. There was almost constant rebellion and warfare. In trying to understand the meaning of life in times that were often cruel and brutal, many Tang poets turned to Taoism. Thinking about the beauties of nature offered an escape from war's horrors. Like the poems of others in his time, many of Li Bai's poems reflect the world he lived in and saw. But even his war poems contain images of the natural world:

Moon over Mountain Pass

A bright moon rising above T'ien Shan
Lost in a vast ocean of clouds.
The long wind, across thousands upon thousands of miles.
Blows past the Jade-gate Pass.
The army of Han has gone down the Pai-teng Road,
As the barbarian hordes probe at Ch'ing-hai Bay.
It is known that from the battlefield
Few ever live to return.
Men at garrison look on the border scene.
Home thoughts deepen sorrow on their faces.
In the towered chambers tonight,
Ceaseless are the women's sighs.

Another of China's greatest poets was Su Dongpo (Su Tong-p'o), who lived during the Song dynasty (960–1279). Su was a Confucian scholar-official who worked for the government. In fact, he gained fame as one of China's finest administrators. He wrote many official documents in clear, practical, Confucian prose. His mother was a Taoist, however, and Su had a Taoist education. As he grew older, he was attracted to Buddhism. These three traditions blended in his poetry. Often, his practical or fatalistic Confucian and Buddhist thoughts are brightened with natural images that reveal his Taoist leanings.

Seeing the Year Out

Do you want to know what the passing year is like?
A snake slithering down a hole.
Half his long scales already hidden,
How to stop him getting away?

Grab his tail and pull, you say? . . .
I get up and look at the slanting Dipper.
How could I hope next year won't come—
My mind shrinks from the failures it may bring.
I work to hold onto the night.
While I can still brag I'm young.

Taoism encouraged a lack of restraint and an openness to beauty that released a creative spirit in many poets. Together with the Taoist sensitivity to the natural world, it left a lasting mark on centuries of Chinese poetry.

Taoism and Painting

Even more than poetry, Chinese painting became an expression of Tao. According to one of the early Taoist paradoxes, Tao could not be expressed by either words or silence. To Taoists, painting helped to explain how that might be possible. Painting is neither words nor silence, yet it communicates ideas and truths about nature and the universe. The poet Su Dongpo, who was also a painter, called paintings "silent poems."

Painting in China began in the temples. Monks and priests drew the patterns of the sun, the moon, and the stars as part of their religious rituals. Later, monks and nuns practiced painting as a devotional exercise. The concentration required for painting was a way of focusing the mind on the harmony of the natural world. Even after its purpose was no longer strictly religious, the basic aim of painting was still to express the Chinese belief in universal order and harmony of Tao.

In the fifth century, a Chinese art critic named Xie Ho (Hsieh Ho) established six canons, or rules, for the creation of truly great art. According to Xie Ho, five of whose canons dealt with technique, form, color, composition, and the preservation of Chinese tradition, a painting must have qi—that is, energy, the breath of life. The sixth canon indicated that qi could not be acquired simply by practice and study; it had to come from within. Thus, Chinese painters looked on painting not as a profession but as a way of life. They worked for years to develop the muscular control necessary to make the sure, swift, delicate strokes that would

明謝樗仙關山雪霽圖

■ *Chinese landscape painters attempted to capture the spirit of a scene rather than a literal representation. In this scroll entitled "Travelers in Mountain Pass after Heavy Snow," the artist has distorted the perspective to create a feeling of dizzying height as the tiny travelers make their way along the precipitous trail toward the top. The vertical shape of the scroll suggests the relationship of heaven and earth and suggests a spiritual journey as well as a physical one.*

infuse their paintings with qi. Xie Ho's rules had set the standards for Chinese art for centuries to come.

The goal of a painter was to reach a level of true inspiration, a union with Tao. Like the meditating monks and nuns of the Taoist monasteries, painters tried to achieve a state in which their hearts and minds were emptied, their spirits freed, and their bodies prepared so that the creative force could work through them.

In one of his poems, Su Dongpo tells of learning to paint from his friend Yuko:

> *When Yuko painted bamboo,*
> *He saw bamboo, not himself.*
> *Nor was he simply unconscious of himself:*
> *Trance-like, he left his body.*
> *His body was transformed into bamboo,*
> *Creating inexhaustible freshness . . .*

The classical painters strove to achieve this union with the subject. A painting was not a literal representation of a scene but a blending of what the artist saw and the way the artist's mind transformed it. The most important factor was that the breath of life should appear in every form.

Wang Wei (699–759) was the landscape painter of his age whose work best captured the essence of qi. A Taoist, he drew strength and inspiration from nature. "Gazing upon the clouds of autumn, my spirit takes wings and soars," he wrote. "Facing the breeze of spring, my thoughts flow like great, powerful currents." He wrote of looking at a well-executed painting: "The wind rises from the green forest, and the foaming water rushes in the stream. Alas! Such painting cannot be achieved by physical movements of the fingers and hand, but only by the spirit entering into them. This is the nature of painting."

The paintings themselves adhered to the principle of yin and yang, the opposing forces that balance each other in the natural world. Landscape painters in particular worked to achieve a perfect balance of elements through composition. Mountains and foothills were balanced by rivers and streams, and long views of land by clouds and trees. Painters hoped to capture the feeling

■ *In the scroll "Early Autumn," the thirteenth-century painter Qian Xuan captures the pulsating life at a pond's edge. The swooping dragonfly and the leaping frog are examples of the Taoist concept of qi, or breath, in Chinese painting.*

of endless change and motion and the cycles of life that were basic to Taoism. In keeping with the principle of qi, they felt that landscapes should never seem still. Paintings were often done on long scrolls that were unrolled a little at a time to display a constantly changing perspective. Tiny figures or buildings in the landscape symbolized the unimportance of human beings in the universe.

"His mountains soared and his springs flowed," it was said of Wang Wei. "To paint mountains," Wang wrote, "one must first know their spiritual forms." His Taoist approach to painting had a profound effect on succeeding generations of artists. A thousand years later in 1701, the classic Chinese how-to book of painting, *Mustard Seed Garden Manual,* held up his style as a model for aspiring painters.

Although Taoist ideals are most clearly expressed in landscape painting, they can be found in other subjects as well. The Chinese are famous for their graceful drawings and paintings of forms in nature. These subjects, like others, were held to the standard of qi, the life force. Whatever they were painting, artists were reminded to set their minds on the harmony of the universe.

The classic style of painting continued to have great influence into the modern age, but other forms of painting also expressed Taoist ideas. In the south of China in the twelfth century, Taoist thought influenced the Chan Buddhists and gave rise to another form of painting.

The Taoist and Chan Buddhist painters believed that inspiration often came in a flash and left as quickly. They turned away from the practiced, thoughtful style of the northern painters and experimented with more spontaneous forms. They drew with whatever was at hand—one artist was said to have used his cap dipped in ink—and finished the details later. A frequent subject was the dragon, a Taoist symbol because of its great force and its magical qualities.

One of those so-called "rapid ink" drawings clearly demonstrates Taoist influence. Entitled "Two Minds in Harmony," it shows an old man asleep, leaning on the back of a sleeping tiger. The painting, which is believed to have been drawn with a bunch of straw dipped in ink, illustrates the basic Taoist belief in the harmony between human beings and nature.

Today, Chinese students of painting still follow the six canons laid down by Xie Ho in the fifth century. They work to acquire the technique of brush strokes, coloration, and form that have governed Chinese painting for centuries, often combining it with rapid-ink and Western techniques. Among China's artists, nature remains a popular subject, still an important element of Chinese culture and part of the Taoist legacy.

Tao and Calligraphy

Chinese painting is closely linked to another ancient art form, that of calligraphy, or the writing of Chinese characters. Both

■ *The irregular natural forms of plants and flowers lend themselves especially well to "rapid ink" drawing, which attempts to capture the essence of a subject in a few swift, spontaneous strokes.*

developed classical styles during the Tang dynasty, and both have many similarities. Since calligraphy and painting use the same materials—brush and ink—and both are based on line and form, many painters practiced calligraphy to help train their hands and eyes for painting. But calligraphy is an art in its own right. Examples of fine Chinese writing are considered valuable works of art today.

Chinese characters are pictographic; originally the characters were simple line drawings of objects. To a calligrapher, every line and dot suggests the form of something in nature. Thus, the natural world is considered an important inspiration for calligraphy.

Calligraphers try to make their writing appear as if it had grown naturally. They attempt to give it qi, which they define as "the kind of life inherent in mountains, streams, and trees." Well-formed characters are said to have "bone" and to be "sinewy." They appear lean and muscular, not flabby and soft, or "dead."

In order for a character to have qi, every stroke in it must convey a sense of living movement. The Chinese feel that looking at a fine piece of calligraphy should be like watching a dancer perform. In both arts, rhythm, line, and form are blended into a harmonious whole that reflects the harmony of the universe.

Each character must also be balanced. Its yin and yang, or weak and strong, elements must fit together into a tightly knit

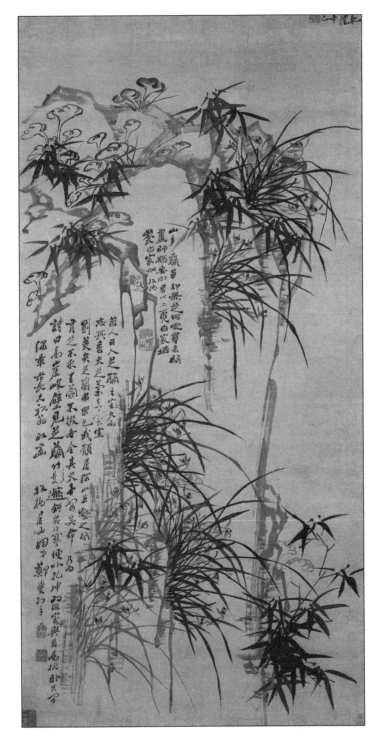

Chinese painters chose bamboo as a subject because its strength, beauty, and grace represent qualities they considered ideal. The different techniques required to render the branches, leaves, knots, and stalks of the bamboo plant are similar to those required for calligraphy.

whole. Along with this, it must be "centered." It is not enough to make perfect strokes; the space between the strokes must be controlled so that the character holds together visually. All of these concepts are closely related to Taoist ideas of balance and harmony.

Fine calligraphy takes many years to learn. In addition to the arm, fingers, and wrist, the whole body is involved in creating and controlling strokes. Manuals on calligraphy explain that the posture must be upright and balanced—calligraphers usually stand when they work—the wrist suspended above the paper, and the mind concentrated. Breathing is controlled, and its energy channeled within the body. In China, calligraphy is considered to be a healthful exercise that contributes to longevity, as physical an activity as tennis or golf.

The discipline needed for calligraphy is similar to that needed for meditation. From at least the fourth century of the common era, Taoist monks learned it as part of their devotional practice and used it to copy sacred texts. It was yet another way of focusing the mind and body on Tao. Even today, calligraphers try to empty their minds and write in a state of mental calm like the tranquillity of the ancient Taoist monks.

Classical calligraphers also turned to the work of still earlier writers for inspiration. Huang Ting Jian (Huang T'ing-chien) (1045–1101) was a calligrapher of the Song period whose work helped to bring new style and vitality to his art. A revolutionary who was forced to endure exile, he used sixth- and eighth-century Taoist texts for models. He believed that copying these texts would be "an elixir that transforms iron into gold," a kind of mental tonic. Huang was described as following through each stroke with his whole body, alternately lifting and pressing down on the brush to form strokes full of individuality and life. The force of his personality combined with ritual and nature to produce work of lasting beauty and power.

In classical Chinese art, calligraphy, painting, and poetry often appear together on one scroll. The interplay between the words in the poem, the design of the characters, and the figures and forms of the painting enrich one another, creating the sense of harmony in the universe that is Tao.

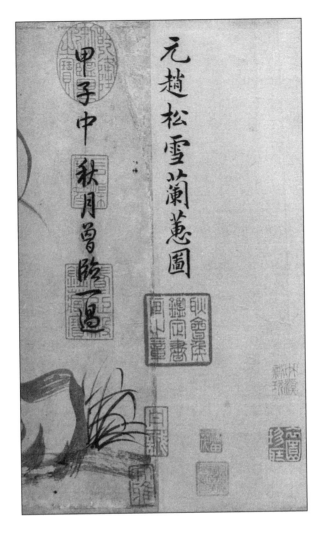

 The Qing emperor Qianlong (Ch'ien Lung) (1735-1795) left behind many examples of calligraphy. Here, his work appears with imperial seals on a scroll by Zhou Mengfu (1254-1322), a master of the graceful and fluid "regular" calligraphy style, which Qianlong tried to emulate.

Taoist Music

In the seventeenth century, painter Wang Yuan-qi wrote, "The Tao or 'way' of music is interchangeable with that of painting." Taoists understood music to be a part of the harmony of the universe. Both instrumental music and song are an essential part of Taoist ritual.

Taoist ritual music varied from sect to sect and from area to area. In some parts of the country, percussion instruments like drums, bells, cymbals, and gongs were favored. Other areas developed traditions using oboes, flutes, and strings, or combinations of percussion and wind instruments.

The ancient Taoist ritual *Zhai Jiao (Chai Chiao)* is used to make offerings to the gods for immortality. The song that accompanies it describes how the gods help people overcome the demons that bring natural disasters. It is played on traditional Chinese musical instruments, including a flute, a two-stringed fiddle, a Chinese mandolin, and a harp. In form and sound, the song merges its own region's Chinese folk music and ballads with imperial court music. It is intended to produce feelings of calm and peace, in keeping with Taoist philosophy.

Traditionally, Taoist music was never written down. It was considered "heavenly music," a ritual form, to be passed on by priests to the next generation of musicians. During China's Cultural Revolution (1966–1976), the government attacked many of China's intellectuals and artists for their views. Taoist music was banned along with all religious practice. Priests and monks were persecuted for practicing religion in any way.

A few Taoist priests defied the ban. They struggled to keep the tradition of Taoist music alive by playing in secret, often in caves or in remote mountain areas. But until recently, the knowledge of Taoist music was in grave danger of dying out. The opening of China to the West, however, brought with it a new interest in Chinese culture, including Taoist music.

Professors of music at Chinese universities have been leading the drive to locate and record Taoist music before the people who know it are gone. They have been videotaping priests who remember the music, now very old men, and making transcripts so that others can learn it. The tradition is being passed on to younger priests and to musicians. The music of some rituals is now available in bookstores in Hong Kong and in China.

A rarity in the past, religious music events are now found throughout China. Taoist music societies often sponsor such gatherings, as do local and provincial governments. The increasing visibility of traditional Chinese music may be due to the reforming Communist government's new religion policy. The government now recognizes traditional religious music as an important part of China's cultural heritage.

The Tao of Dance

Like music, dance is also a part of Taoist ritual. Priests follow the traditional patterns of ancient dances as they chant Taoist liturgy. The circling movements of the ritual dances are believed to bring worshipers into harmony with the natural cycles of the universe. These "magic circles" are repeated in ritual swordplay, in which the priest or master wields a sword to drive away evil spirits, and in the graceful movements of taijiquan, both of which have devotional value for the Taoist.

Taoism and Artistic Expression

For centuries, Taoism has been linked with the creative forces of the natural world. It has always encouraged freedom and individuality, a close observation and acceptance of nature, a sense of harmony, and an awareness of beauty. In addition, it has stressed disciplines that channel vitality and energy along creative lines. Taoists have always been among China's finest artists and poets. Their contributions have greatly enriched Chinese culture.

In the past decade, the Western world had begun to examine the Taoist principles of concentration, relaxation, and physical training to enhance performance in the arts. Both Chinese and Western painters, singers, players of musical instruments, and other artists, are exploring ancient Taoist practices to give their work qi, or energy. In so doing, they parallel the efforts of Taoists to control and direct the energy of the natural universe in everyday life.

CHAPTER 7

Taoism
Yesterday, Today,
and Tomorrow

Throughout its long tradition in China, Taoism's fate has ebbed and flowed. Periods of influence were followed by ages of repression. Despite times of imperial patronage, Taoism was usually on the outside of official channels of power, and sometimes in the opposition. If Confucianism was the religion of official China, then Taoism was the religion of unofficial China, the "religion of the people." In its long history, Taoism has often been on the verge of extinction. The twentieth century marked another challenging period in Taoism's storied history.

In 1911, the last Chinese empire fell. In the new republic that replaced it the role of religion and traditional Chinese thought was unclear. Some believed that the best of China's ancient culture deserved re-appropriation and scrutiny, while others were convinced that China's only hope lay in imitating the West. As part of the movement for national renewal in 1917, all property of state religious organizations was confiscated in what became known as the "Fourth May Movement." Many temples were ruined. Other similar programs effectively destroyed temples throughout China in the decade that

followed. By the 1930s, great political forces were presenting further challenges to the region. Imperial Japan invaded China in 1937, destroying Taoist temples, priceless ancient literature, and artifacts.

The tumult of the Japanese invasion, then that of the Second World War, was soon followed by the 1949 Communist takeover. Led by Mao Zedong, the Communists made no secret of their disdain for all religion. By the 1950s it was possible for one Chinese scholar to assert Taoism's certain extinction: its vitality was sapped, its schools were in decline, its priesthood was disorganized, it lacked organization and a social program, and, dominated by the search for earthly blessings, it had lost its vision. Taoism's influence, in the opinion of many, had been reduced to art, rituals, and festivals.

We now know in retrospect that early twentieth century forecasts of Taoism's imminent demise were exaggerated. China has been ravaged by war and revolutions, and its inhabitants have often been caught in the middle of powerful forces largely beyond their control. Despite all this, as in ages past, Taoism has survived. Now into a new century, its future is in no way assured. Yet there are hopeful signs that after a turbulent and destructive era, Taoism is enjoying a period of renewal and restoration. Taoist centers once closed are re-opening; temples once destroyed are being rebuilt; teachings thought lost forever only twenty years ago are being passed on to a new generation. The Chinese government's new policy toward religion, adopted in 1979, promises continued growth for religion in China, including Taoism. In the West, Taoism in its traditional form and in the sciences it produced is finding new adherents.

Taoism Under Communism

After World War II, China was seized by a violent civil war between the Nationalist government and Communist rebels. In 1949, Mao and the Communists emerged victorious, establishing the People's Republic. The Nationalists fled to the island of Taiwan. As we will see, even while Taoism appeared to diminish in the mainland after 1949, it continued as before, unthreatened, in Taiwan.

■ *Chairman Mao Zedong reads the proclamation of the founding of the People's Republic of China in Tienanmen Square on October 1, 1949. During his three decades in power, Mao attempted to systematically eliminate all religion in China.*

In the eyes of the Communists, religion was an "opiate of the people," unscientific and therefore outdated. Religion was largely suppressed, perceived as a potential threat to the state and a subversive influence over the people. As a result, all religious affairs in China were placed under the Chinese Communist Party. In 1954, the Religious Affairs Bureau (RAB) was created to supervise all religious activities. Three years later, the Chinese Taoist Association was formed to regulate the religious life of Chinese Taoists.

In the 1950s during the Land Reform movement, Taoist temples lost much of their property, which weakened them economically. Both Taoist and Buddhist monks and nuns were expelled from the remaining monasteries and temples and forced into labor camps. As part of the Great Leap Forward of 1958, ancient and priceless artifacts like temple bells and cauldrons were melted down to produce steel for a country crazy to modernize at nearly any cost. Almost all the temples that survived were requisitioned as army barracks or government offices, or became factories, workshops, or grain stores. Most festivals, all acts of worship, and even the burning of incense were officially forbidden by the government; these things were dismissed as mere superstition. The anti-Taoist policies of the Communists proved frighteningly effective: a decade after the Communist takeover, the number of Taoist monks had been reduced from five million to 50,000.

The situation worsened during the Cultural Revolution, a decade-long campaign designed by Mao Zedong to re-instill the revolutionary fervor of the past, to destabilize the then entrenched Chinese Communist Party, and finally to root out traditional Chinese culture. Ardent young Maoists called Red Guards went on a nationwide rampage. Youth were exhorted to denounce the so-called "Four Olds": old customs, old culture, old habits, and old thinking. Taoists were tortured, killed, or sent off to labor camps. With rare exception, almost all the Taoist centers were destroyed and its surviving followers were scattered. Beginning in 1965, the Cultural Revolution seemed to complete the destruction that earlier anti-religious crusades had begun.

Taoism Under the Religious Freedom Clause

Deng Xiaoping, Mao's successor, ushered in a new era of social and cultural change under the banner of "Reform and Opening." The Religious Freedom Clause of the 1982 constitution now allows for the "right of religious belief." Religion in a rapidly modernizing China is now said to share the same goals of the Communist state: morality, ethics, loyalty to China, and increased productivity. The religious reforms have had the effect of reviving religious practices throughout the country. However, the government continues to maintain a tight grip on religion and still suppresses many groups, ever fearful that they might threaten the stability of the government and the nation if left unchecked.

As odd as it may sound, until the new era ushered in by Deng Xiaoping, few really knew if Taoism had survived the Cultural Revolution. China, as in ages past, had become mostly closed to the West. We now know that Taoism is experiencing a

renaissance. Beginning in the 1980s, temples and monasteries were re-opened, first to tourists, then to their priests and nuns, for proper religious use. Taoist religious leaders were called out of retirement or were allowed to leave the work camps they had been forced into during the Cultural Revolution. New fundraising initiatives were started in China and abroad to rebuild Taoist centers throughout China. The Chinese Taoist Association, dissolved during the Cultural Revolution, was re-established in 1983. One year later, the Baiyun (White Cloud) Temple, the largest Taoist temple in northern China, was reopened. Such restorative activities continued into the 1990s and persist today. While the number of re-opened or re-built temples is still a fraction of what once existed, many of these places are now bustling with activity.

■ *Taoists at a temple in Kunming, Yunnan province. After years of neglect, many temples like this one are slowly being renovated and returned to clergy for their proper religious use.*

Taoism Beyond the People's Republic

Taoism is not confined to the People's Republic of China. Taoists can be found in Cambodia among the ethnic Chinese

Taoist worshipers in Hong Kong make offerings. Taoist practice remained in Hong Kong while the religion's adherents were being persecuted in Communist China. Now that Hong Kong has been reunited to the reforming People's Republic, Taoists can worship as freely as they did when the British governed Hong Kong.

population. In Singapore, thirteen percent of the country's 2.6 million describe themselves as Taoists. Recently, Singaporean Taoist leaders proclaimed Laozi's birthday, the fifteenth day of the second lunar month, "Taoist Day," with the hope that the celebration will catch on among Taoists throughout the world.

Until 1997, Hong Kong was a colony of the United Kingdom. Many feared that the handover of control to Communist China would limit religious freedom, but this has not been the case. The Chinese Taoist Association identifies seventy local groups and more than seven hundred people under its jurisdiction. The Association promotes Taoism through support of the education of children and adults, sponsors Taoist functions throughout Hong Kong, and supports the growth and development of Taoism on the mainland. As in other parts of China, there are many Taoist groups and practices, and Taoism is often practiced together with Buddhism and/or Confucianism. Taoist and Buddhist deities are present in six hundred Chinese temples in Hong Kong.

Taoism's strongest presence outside mainland China is in Taiwan. During the Cultural Revolution, the island was the most visible center for open Taoist practice. The home-in-exile of the Celestial Master, the island boasts three million followers. With such a thriving Taoist community, Taiwan has long been a center of Taoist study, exchange, and scholarship.

Taoism in the West

Although Taoism has not been as popular as Buddhism and Confucianism outside of Asia, there are now Taoist communities in nearly every major Western city. The increased presence of Eastern religions among native Westerners comes at a time when many are looking beyond the traditional religions of the Occident. Eager to seek new answers to old questions, they are often more receptive to these faiths and philosophies than they are to the religions of their parents or grandparents. In a shrinking world, where Taoists meditate in North America and Roman Catholics worship in Korea, the very terms "East" and "West" are not as clear as they once were.

An example of Western Taoism can be found in Weston, Massachusetts. The Center of Traditional Taoist studies is led by a Western master who regularly conducts rituals in a temple filled with traditional Taoists deities. Courses are taught in Taoist religion, philosophy, taijiquan, and martial arts. The Center is recognized by the ancient White Cloud Temple of Shanghai and by Shanghai Quan Shen Taoists, a significant affirmation of its authenticity. Such places are still few in number, but their presence reflects both Western interest in Taoism, and the growth of religious pluralism in North America, where some 30,000 people identify themselves as Taoists.

While the number of Western Taoist initiates remains small, interest in Taoistic techniques and practices is increasing. When one goes to the "Eastern Religions" section of a

Western practitioners of taijiquan alleviate stress in an American hay field. Once an oddity, an increasing number of Westerners are adopting Taoist practices for their health and well-being. Taiji, acupuncture, and herbal medicine are becoming increasingly popular outside of Asia.

neighborhood bookstore today, he or she will see books dealing with the Tao of science, singing, or health. Fritjof Capra's 1975 publication of the *Tao of Physics* began this trend. Capra examines the similarities between physics and Taoism, both disciplines that try to understand the natural laws of the universe. Another intriguing book is the *Tao of Pooh* by Benjamin Hoff. One may be surprised to find out that A.A. Milne's Winnie the Pooh is the prototypical Taoist! Pooh's simplicity, contentment, compassion, and wisdom make him the perfect Western embodiment of the *Tao Te Ching*. Such books represent attempts to apply Taoist concepts to modern Western life.

Over the last thirty years Taoism has influenced the West through the growing popularity of Asian medicine, especially taijiquan, acupuncture, and herbal therapies. In general, Asian medicine is characterized by its attention to the whole person, rather than to localized symptoms, as is often the case in traditional Western medicine.

Scholars consider taiji the ancestor of all Chinese martial arts. Because it involves stretching and extension exercises, it is useful to people of all ages and physical conditions. Many Westerners now practice taiji because they find that it reduces body pains, alleviates tension, and improves circulation.

Acupuncture is another medical art with Taoist roots that is having an increasing influence on Western society. Acupuncturists insert tiny needles into the surface of the body to improve physiological functions. Like taijiquan, acupuncture is based on the assumption that the body is animated by qi, or energy, and that blockages to this energy produce illness. Acupuncture aims to restore equilibrium, the proper flow, and continuity to the flow of qi through manipulation of the meridians (pathways of energy) in the body. Over the last decade, the Western medical community has acknowledged acupuncture's effectiveness in the alleviation of pain, but there is still reluctance to admit its success in treating arthritis, depression, and nicotine addiction— other ailments that acupuncturists commonly treat. In some states in the United States, only medical doctors are allowed to practice acupuncture.

It is no longer unusual to find an herbal medicine section at the local grocery store. What many do not realize when they buy ginkgo biloba or gensing is that such treatments have their roots in Asia. Western science still categorizes herbal medicines as "untested." However, in the years ahead it is likely that Taoism-developed medical arts will become more common and will be incorporated into traditional Western therapies. Seventeen universities in the United States already offer courses in Asian medicine, and many other schools from the West Coast to the East are dedicated to what is often termed complementary and alternative medicine.

Taoism into the Future

We began this chapter noting Taoism's storied past, but what might Taoism look like in the years ahead? Because most have been wrong in their religious predictions, perhaps we should resist the temptation to pass quick judgments or to offer simplistic prophesies. The best way to forecast Taoism's future is probably to observe what is taking place today. Fueled by the liberalizing policies of the People's Republic of China, temples and monasteries throughout the mainland are being rebuilt, attendance at Taoist festivals in China are the highest they have been in three generations, and Taoist masters are emerging from exile to teach interested new disciples the ancient ways of the Celestial Masters.

Fifty years ago Taoism was declared dead, due in part to the decline of its schools. Today, Taoist studies take place in religious organizations like the Chinese Taoist Association, in institutions of higher learning like Beijing University, in research institutes like the Chinese Academy of Social Sciences, and in cultural and artistic institutions like the Ethnology Institute. Fifty years ago, the Taoist priesthood was deemed disorganized. Since 1979, the few elderly Taoists still living have begun the process of educating new followers, restoring ancient manuscripts, and reorganizing monastic life. Despite obstacles, they have been largely successful in creating a network of cooperation throughout Asia and the West. Fifty years ago, most Westerners knew almost nothing of Taoism or its constituent arts. Today, as we have seen, there is widespread interest in the *Tao Te Ching* and the *I Ching*; many seek the benefits of Asian medicine and taijiquan; and Taoist organizations in North America are working to preserve and restore China's Taoist heritage. These are promising signs, and a helpful indicator of Taoism's continued renewal in the new century.

Of course, Taoist history, like Taoist teaching, reminds us that times of hardship will naturally follow prosperity. The future is in no way certain. The Communist government still supervises all the religions of China, and often represses "unofficial" groups it deems potentially subversive and unpatriotic. While the government claims that Taoism shares its goals, in truth, it is more accurate to say that the government allows "the people's religion" as long as it appears to support the government's agenda. This agenda could quickly change.

While scores of temples are being rebuilt and others are being handed back to priests, many more remain government offices, workshops, or factories. Historic Taoist centers like Mount Mao near Nanjing—places destroyed, rebuilt, and destroyed again over the last three centuries—now face a new enemy: uncontrolled tourism. While visitors provide the monks and nuns with their main source of income, they also threaten their ability to continue an ascetical lifestyle. Those centers not returned to the masters are often transformed into theme parks.

Like many Chinese intellectuals a century ago, many Chinese now reject religious aspects of Taoism as backward. Young people, eager to embrace the benefits of China's new economy, are often unwilling to embrace a life of contemplation and self-denial. As a result, ancient knowledge, practices, and skills will die with old Taoist practitioners, forever lost because there was simply no one to receive them.

For now, at least, Taoism is enjoying a period of renewal. Against incredible odds, and despite wars, suppression, killing, and scorn, Taoism has survived. It is a startling reality, perhaps best captured by these verses from *Tao Te Ching*:

> *Nothing in the world*
> *is as soft and yielding as water.*
> *Yet for dissolving the hard and inflexible,*
> *Nothing can surpass it.*
> *The soft overcomes the hard;*
> *The gentle overcomes the rigid.*

CHAPTER NOTES

pages 8–9   "Look, and it can't be seen. ..." Stephen Mitchell, *Tao Te Ching: A New English Version.*

page 24   "True mastery can be gained ..." Stephen Mitchell, *Tao Te Ching: A New English Version.*

page 26   "When an archer is shooting for nothing, ..." *Chuang Tzu,* original manuscript.

page 27   "Khing, the master carver, made a bell stand ..." Chuang Tzu, original manuscript.

page 58   "The Tao that can be told ..." Stephen Mitchell, *Tao Te Ching: A New English Version.*

page 59   "Tao has reality and evidence but no action and form. It may be ..." Ch'u Chai and Winberg Chai, *The Story of Chinese Philosophy.*

page 59   "The Tao gives birth to one ..." Stephen Mitchell, *Tao Te Ching: A New English Version.*

pages 61–62   "Tao can be concise, but stretched quite long: dark, but shine ..." *Huainanzi,* original manuscript.

page 64   "... one who starts out with this early life as all we can or ..." Lin Yutang, *The Importance of Living.*

page 66   "Fill your bowl to the brim ..." Stephen Mitchell, *Tao Te Ching: A New English Version"*

page 66   "When you realize where you come from, ..." Stephen Mitchell, *Tao Te Ching: A New English Version.*

page 78   "The Tao gives birth to one, ..." Stephen Mitchell, *Tao Te Ching: A New English Version.*

page 89   "Our beloved daughter, sister of [brothers' names] will this day..." Michael R. Saso, *Blue Dragon, White Tiger: Taoist Rites of Passage.*

page 96   "I have built my hut beside a busy road ..." Alasdair Clayre, *The Heart of the Dragon.*

page 97   "You ask me: ..." Molly Joel Coye and Jon Livingston, eds., translated by Cyril Birch, *China, Yesterday and Today.*

page 98   "Moon over Mountain Pass," translated by Joseph J. Lee.

pages 98–99   "Seeing the Year Out," Burton Watson, *Translations from a Song Dynasty Poet,* from Alasdair Clayre, *The Heart of the Dragon.*

page 101   "When Yuko painted bamboo, ..." *Su Shi, Collected Poems,* from Alasdair Clayre, *The Heart of the Dragon.*

page 121   "Nothing in the world is as soft. ..." Stephen Mitchell, *Tao Te Ching: A New English Version.*

GLOSSARY

Alchemy—A philosophy, blending science, magic, and religion, in which its practitioners attempted to turn common materials into gold. *see also* **Elixir of life; Spiritual alchemy**

Ba Xian—The Eight Immortals; a group of Taoist gods, formerly historical figures and heroes, who could be called on to help people in need.

Calligraphy—The art of fine handwriting. In China, the writing of Chinese characters by hand with a fine brush; also in China, considered a branch of the art of painting.

Daocang—*see* **Tao Ts'ang**

Elixir of life—In early Taoism, a much sought after "golden potion" that would ensure immortality, or eternal life. Taoist alchemists believed that if gold could be produced from common materials, a potion could then be developed that would ensure long life or immortality. *see also* **Alchemy**

Ghost money—A paper-printed representation of money, symbolizing family wealth, designed to be burned as an offering to the gods.

Heavenly worthy—A celestial being, either god or immortal; one of the Three Pure Ones, the gods of heaven, earth, and human beings.

Immortal—A person who achieved perfection and rose to the Highest Purity Heaven of the Taoists, spiritually as well as physically. *see also* **Xian**

Jiao—Literally, an offering; a basic Taoist ritual, simple or elaborate, conducted for many reasons, but primarily for the welfare of living people.

Jing—Literally, vitality; associated with creativity and the basic functions of the body, including procreation. In Taoism, one of the three treasures of human life; *see also* **Qi; Shen**

Libation—A liquid, usually wine, poured as an offering in a religious ceremony.

Libationer—An early Taoist priest.

Mao Shan—Mount Mao, one of Taoism's five sacred mountains; site of the birth of the Highest Purity sect, or the Mao Shan school of Taoism.

Oratory—A place of Taoist worship, overseen by a priest called a libationer.

Qi—Literally, the breath of life; physical energy, the essence of life, control of which is essential for longevity and for harmony with Tao. In Taoism, one of the three treasures of human life; *see also* **Jing; Shen**

Qigong—Breath control, a Taoist ritual practiced to enhance religious devotion.

Quanzhen—The Complete Reality movement, a school of Taoism marked by a return to the natural and free way of life in early Taoism.

Shen—Literally, spirit, or that part of a human being that controls thought, intellect, and spirituality. In Taoism, one of the three treasures of human life. *see also* **Jing; Qi**

Spiritual alchemy—The blending of body, mind, and spirit through meditation and the practice of good health to achieve longevity.

Tai Shan—Mount Tai, one of Taoism's five sacred mountains.

Taijiquan—A system of exercise developed by Taoists to help people channel the flow of qi, or energy, within their bodies during meditation. *see also* **Qi**

Tao (Dao)—Literally, the Way; the nameless force behind all things.

Tao Jia—Taoist thought; the philosophy of Taoism.

Tao Jiao—The religion of Taoism.

Tao Te Ching (Daodejing)—The *Laozi*, the Book of the Way and Its Power; the basic writings of Taoism, attributed to Laozi.

Tao Ts'ang (Daocang)—The Taoist *Canon*, or sacred writings.

Taocracy—A state or community organized around the Taoist religion.

Three Pure Ones—Heavenly Worthies, the three highest gods of Taoism, who, together, embody all aspects of the Tao.

Way of the Celestial Masters—Tien Shi, the Taoist sect established by Zhang Dao Ling, the founder of religious Taoism.

Wuwei—The taoist philosophy of "non-doing"; the practice of being aligned with nature, which allows one to accomplish things without effort.

Xian—The state of immortality. *see* **Immortal**

Yin and yang—In Chinese philosophy, the inseparable opposing forces of the universe, whose balance creates harmony. Yin is negative, dark, female, quiet; yang is positive, light male, active. One cannot exist without the other.

Zi—Literally, master or teacher; a title of respect.

FOR FURTHER READING

Capra, Fritjof. *The Tao of Physics,* 4th ed. Boston: Shambhala, 2000.

Chai, Ch'u, and Wineberg Chai. *The Story of Chinese Philosophy.* New York: Washington Square Press, 1961.

Ching, Julia. *Chinese Religions.* London: Macmillan; Maryknoll, New York: Orbis Books, 1993.

Clayre, Alasdair. *The Heart of the Dragon.* Boston: Houghton Mifflin, 1984.

Dingbo, Wu, and Patrick D. Murphy, eds. *Handbook of Chinese Popular Culture.* Westport, Conn. and London: Greenwood Publishing Group, 1994.

Dreher, Diane. *The Tao of Inner Peace,* rev. ed. New York: Plume, 2000.

Hoff, Benjamin. *The Tao of Pooh.* New York: Penguin Books, 1982.

Kohn, Livia. *Daoism and Chinese Culture.* Cambridge, Mass.: Three Pines Press, 2001.

Mitchell, Stephen. *Tao Te Ching: A New English Version, with Forward and Notes.* New York: Harper and Row, Publishers, 1988.

Paper, Jordon, and Laurence G. Thompson, ed. *Chinese Way in Religion,* 2nd ed. Belmont, Calif.: Wadsworth Publishing Company, 1997.

Robinet, Isabelle. *Taoism: Growth of a Religion,* translated by Phyllis Brooks. Stanford: Stanford University Press, 1997.

Saso, Michael R. *Blue Dragon, White Tiger: Taoist Rites of Passage.* Hawaii: University of Hawaii Press, 1990.

Schipper, Kristofer. *The Taoist Body,* trans. by Karen C. Duval. Berkeley: University of California Press, 1994.

Sommer, Deborah, ed. *Chinese Religion: An Anthology of Sources.* New York: Oxford University Press, 1997.

Thompson, Laurence G. *Chinese Religion: An Introduction,* 5th ed. Belmont, Calif.: Wadsworth Publishing Company, 1995.

Wong, Eva. *The Shambhala Guide to Taoism.* Boston and London: Shambhala, 1997.

Wong, Eva, ed. and trans. *Teachings of the Tao: Readings from the Taoist Spiritual Tradition.* Boston and London: Shambhala, 1997.

Yutang, Lin. *The Importance of Living.* New York: William Morrow, 1998.

INDEX

Acupuncture 118, 119
Alchemy, discouragement of 48; immortality and 31; science and 32–33; spiritual 43, 48, 92
Altars, domestic ritual and 81
Ancestor Lu. *see* Lu Yan
Ancestor rites 81–82
Ancestors 67; altars to 81; wedding rituals and 89

Baopuzi ("He Who Holds to Simplicity") 43
Ba Xian (Eight Immortals) 18, 38, 68–71
Birth, rituals associated with 87
Blue Heaven 37, 39
Body, diet and 10–11; harmony of 9; health of 10–12
"Book of the Way and Its Power, The." *see Tao Te Ching*
Breath. *see* Qi, Qigong
Buddhism 12, 13; attempts to combine with Confucianism and Taoism 45, 54; number of followers of 6; spread of 39; in Yuan dynasty 52

Calendar, Chinese 82; of festivals 84–86; Reign of the Forgiver of Sins 84–86; Reign of the Spirits of Heaven 84–86; Reign of the Water Spirits 84–86. *see also* Festivals
Calligraphy 45, 88, 103–106; qi and 104
Canon 49, 56–58; revision of 58
Cao Cao (Ts'ao Ts'ao) 42–43
Celestials 67, 68, 120
Chai Chaio (Zhai Jiao) 108
Chan Buddhist painters 103
Chang Chueh. *see* Zhang Zhue
Chang Tao Ling. *see* Zhang Dao Ling
Chen Tsung (Zhen Cong) 49
Ch'i. *see* Qi
Ch'ien Lung (Qianlong) 107
Children, rituals related to 87–88
China, dynasties of 18, 30, 51; Golden Age of Philosophy 18; religions of 12; Religious Affairs Bureau 113 (RAB); Religious Freedom Clause of 1982 114–115; spread of Taoism

and 6–8. *see also* Calendar; People's Republic of China
Chinese Academy of Social Sciences 120
Chinese language, calligraphy and 104–106; names 40; Pinyin writing 12; translating from 60
Chinese Taoist Association 113, 115, 116, 120
Ch'ing dynasty. *see* Qing dynasty
Ch'in dynasty. *see* Qin dynasty
Chou dynasty. *see* Zhou dynasty
Christianity, spread of, in China 54–55
Chuang Tzu. *see* Zhuangzi
Chung-li. *see* Zhung Li
Communism 55, 112–115
Complete Reality Taoism. *see* Quanzhen
Confucianism 12, 13, 19–22; appeal of 19–20; attempts to fuse with Buddhism and Taoism 54; criticism of 20; harmony in 19; history of 6; ideal society 19; moral behavior 19; Taoist influence on 49; under Ming dynasty 52; under Tang dynasty 47
Confucius 18–22
Cultural Revolution 108, 114, 115

Da Cheng Jiao (Ta Ch'eng Chia) 54
Daocang. see Tao Ts'ang
Daodejing. see Tao Te Ching
Dao Hong Jing (Tao Hung Ching) 45–46
Daoism 12. *see also* Taoism
Dao Qian (T'ao Ch'ien) 96
Da Xue (Ta Hsueh) 54
Demons. *see* Kuei
Devotional exercise 53
Diet 10–11
Di Kuai Li 38, 69
Divination 85–87
Division of Lamps ritual 77–78
Domestic rituals 67, 80–81; Kitchen God 67, 85, 118
Dragon-Tiger Mountain (Lung Hu Shan) 49, 55, 67, 121
Drowned souls 79–80

Earth God 85

Earthly Branches 82
Eastern Han dynasty 51
Eight Immortals. *see* Ba Xian
Energy. *see* Qi
Ethnology Institute 120
Evil spirits, exorcism of 80
Exercise. *see* Taijiquan

Festivals 82–87; calendar of 84–86; Festival of Earth Spirits 85; New Year's Day 83–84; Reign of the Forgiver of Sins 84–86; Reign of the Spirits of Heaven 84–86; Reign of the Water Spirits 84–86; Tomb Sweeping Festival 81. *see also* Calendar; Ritual
Five Classics 19, 54
Five Dynasties 51
Five Elements 82
Floating of the Water Lamps 79–80, 85
Fourth May Movement 110
Funerals, rituals associated with 89–91

Genghis Khan 50
Gods 49; Earth God 85; God of Agriculture 71; God of Land 71; God of Stoves 67; Kitchen God 67, 85, 118; mountain gods 67; personal 71–73; popular belief in 67–68; visualizing, as meditation 92–93; Water God 85
Go Hong (Ko Hung) 43
Golden potion 31–32
Government, advice on 24; philosophy of 34–36, 37; Taoism and 46, 120
"Great Learning" 54
"Great Peace." *see* Taiping

Han dynasty 29, 37; Eastern 51; failure of 42; Taoist rebellion against 37–39; Western 30
Han Xiang Zi 38, 69
Han Zhung Li 18, 38, 69, 71
Harmony 8, 9, 61–63; in Confucianism 19; in paintings 103; universe and 59
Healing 41

Health, physical 10–12
Heavenly shadow-boxing 118. *see also* Taijiquan
Heavenly worthies 68
Hermits 20, 97. *see also* Immortals; Mountain men; Sages
Heroes 67–68, 71
"He Who Holds to Simplicity." *see Baopuzi*
Highest Purity Taoists 45, 46, 55, 56; under Song dynasty 48–49; under Tang dynasty 47–48
Ho Chi Minh City, Vietnam 58
Homeless souls, ritual of Universal Salvation and 79
Hong Xiu Zhuan (Hung Hsiueh Chuan) 38, 54–55
Hsieh Ho. *see* Xie Ho
Huainanzi ("Masters of Huainan") 30–33, 61–62
Huang Di (Yellow Emperor) 16–18, 31, 68
Huang Ting Jian (Huang T'ing-chien) 106
Hung Hsiueh Chuan. *see* Hong Xiu Zhuan

I Ching. see Yijing
Immortality 64; alchemy and 31; elixirs and 31–32, 48; music and 108; spiritual alchemy and 43; Zhang Dao Ling and 42; xian 11–12
Immortals 11–12, 31; Eight Immortals 18, 38, 68–71; as folk heroes 48; sages 64
Importance, unimportance of 24–25, 63
Infancy, rituals associated with 87–88

Jade Emperor. *see* Ling Pao
Japanese, destruction of Taoist temples 112
Jiao (offering) 76–79, 88. *see also* Ritual
Jin dynasty 51

Kitchen God 67, 85
Kuei (demons) 73, 108

Landscape painting 101–103
Laozi 20–22, 47, 58, 62, 67, 68; birth-day 48, 116; criticism of Confucius by 21–22; explanation of, by Zhuangzi 26–27; spirit appears to Kou Zhen Qi 46; spirit appears to Zhang Dao Ling 39–40; *Tai shang Lao jun* 41
Legendary period 30
Liang dynasty 45–46
Li Bai. *see* Li Po
Li Ehr 21, 47. *see also* Laozi
Ling Pao (Jade Emperor) 49, 68
Li Po (Li Bai) 97–98
Literature 94–99
Liu An 29–33
Lost souls, liberation of 85; rituals for 79–80
Lu Dongbin. *see* Lu Tong Pin)
Lung Hu Shan (Dragon-Tiger Mountain) 49, 55, 67, 121
Lu Tong Pin. *see* Lu Dongbin
Lu Yan (Ancestor Lu) 50, 69–71

Manchus 53–54
Mao Shan school 45–46, 55, 56; under Tang dynasty 47–48
"Masters of Huainan." *see Huainanzi*
Mastery, Zhuangzi's explanation of 27–28
Meditation 11, 91–93; breath control 92, 118; exercise and 92; Highest Purity Taoists and 45; longevity and 11; visualizing gods and 92–93; in the West 119
Ming dynasty 51, 52–53
Moral behavior 13, 15; in Confucianism 19
Mother spirit (chuang mu) 88
Mountain men 20, 97. *see also* Hermits; Immortals; Sages
Mount Mao 55, 121. *see also* Mao Shan school
Music 95–96, 97, 107–108

Names, in Chinese language 40
Nature 63–64; landscape painting 101–103; observation of 20
New Year's Day 83–84
Non-doing. *see* Wuwei

One 59

Oratories 41
Orphan souls 73

Painting, calligraphy 103–106; as Taoist expression 99–103
People's Republic of China, establishment of 55; Pinyin writing 12; Taoism in 8
Perfection, Zhuangzi's explanation of 27–28
Personal gods 71–73
Pinyin 12, 40
Poets and poetry 96–99
Popular Taoism 67. *see also* Religious Taoism
Psychological healing 41
Pure Ones 68; New Year's Day and 83; ritual and 77–79

Qi (ch'i) (breath or energy) 11, 65–66; acupuncture and 118–119; calligraphy and 104; creativity and 109; exercise and 65–66; meditation and 119; painting and 99, 102, 103
Qigong (breath control) 92, 118
Qin (Ch'in) dynasty 29, 30
Qing (Ch'ing) dynasty 51, 53–54
Qiu Zhang-jun (Ch'iu Chang Chun) 50
Quanzhen (Complete Reality Taoism) 49–50

Redhead Taoists 76
Reign of the Forgiver of Sins 84–86
Reign of the Spirits of Heaven 84–86
Reign of the Water Spirits 84–86
Religious Taoism. *see* Tao jia
Return to Unity ritual 78–79
Rites of passage 87–91; birth and infancy 87–88; funerals 89–91; weddings 88–89
Rituals, ancestor 81–82; dance 109; defined 74; Division of the Lamps 77–78; domestic 67, 80–81, 85; exorcism 80; Floating of the Water Lamps 79–80, 85; importance of 74; jiao 76–79, 88; for lost souls 79–80; Return to Unity 78–79; rites of passage 87–91; of Universal Salvation 79. *see also* Festivals

Sexagenary Cycle 82
Shang dynasty 18, 30
Sheng Mu 71–73
Shen (spirit) 65, 67–68, 89
Shrines 85–87
Song dynasty 51; fall of 49; Taoism under 48–49
Souls, of the drowned 79–80; homeless 79; lost 79–80, 85
Spirit. *see* Shen
Spiritual alchemy 43, 48, 92
Spiritual healing 41
Su Dongpo (Su Tong-p'o) 98–99, 101
Sui dynasty 51
Su Tong-p'o. *see* Su Dongpo

Taijiquan (t'ai chi ch'uan) (exercise) 11, 53, 88, 118, 119, 120; devotional 53; meditation and 92; qi and 65–66
Taiping ("Great Peace") 37, 54–55
Taiwan 8, 55, 112, 117
Tai Wu Di, Emperor 46
Tang dynasty 46–48, 51, 96–98
Tang Xuan-cong 58
Tao, Chinese character for 9; harmony with 8; as ultimate reality 58–59; understanding 24–25
T'ao Ch'ien. *see* Dao Qian
Taocracy 41–43
Tao Hung Ching. *see* Dao Hong Jing
Taoism, attempts to combine Confucianism and Buddhism with 54; beliefs 8–12; Buddhism and 45, 54; communism and 55, 112–114, 115–116, 120; Confucianism and 18–22, 49; future of 119–121; government and 34–36, 46, 120; history of 6, 16–18; in modern age 55, 110–121; moral behavior 13, 15; number of followers of 6; reform of 46; as religion 39–40; repression of 33, 36, 52, 55, 112, 113–114; restoration of 112, 114–115; spelling of 12; spread of 6–8, 26, 116–120; in

Taiwan 8, 112, 116–118; under Song dynasty 48–49; under Tang dynasty 46–48; under Yuan dynasty 52; varieties of 13, 15; in the West 117–119. *see also* Highest Purity Taoists; Religious Taoism; Way of the Celestial Masters
Tao jia (religious Taoism) 67; development of 39–40; early 36–37; founding of 40
Tao of Physics, The (Capra) 118
Tao of Pooh 118
Tao Te Ching (Daodejing) ("The Book of the Way and Its Power") 22–25, 31, 58, 59, 66; government philosophy in 34, 37; as literature 96, 121; meditation and 91–92; perfect society in 37; ritual and 78; translating 60; under Tang dynasty 48; West and 118, 120; as work of deified Laozi 41
Tao Ts'ang (Daocang) 49, 56–58; domestic ritual and 81, 82
Temples 8, 85–87, 115
Three Kingdoms dynasty 51, 71
Three Pure Ones 68; New Year's Day and 83; ritual and 77–79
Three treasures 65–66
Tien, New Year's Day and 83
Tien Shi ("Way of the Celestial Masters") 41, 42, 43, 46, 49, 56, 121
Ts'ao Ts'ao. *see* Cao Cao

Ultimate Reality 8, 26
Unimportance 24–25, 63
Universal Salvation, ritual of 79

Valley spirit 63
Vitality (jing, or ching) 65

Wade-Giles, names 40
Water God 85

Way of the Celestial Masters. *see* Tien Shi
Weddings, rituals associated with 88–89
Wei dynasty 42–43
Western Han dynasty 30
Western Taoism 117–119; and Asian medicine 119; Center of Traditional Taoist Studies 117; techniques and practices 117
Wu Di, Emperor 45–46
Wuwei (non-doing) 11, 61; Zhuangzi's explanation of 28–29, 97

Xian. *see* Immorality, Immortals
Xiaoping, Deng 114
Xie Ho (Hsieh Ho) 99–101, 103

Yang, great 61; New Year's Day and 83. *see also* Yin and yang
Yang Xi (Yang Hsi) 43–46, 48
Yellow Emperor. *see* Huang Di
Yellow Heaven 37, 39
Yijing (I Ching) 54, 120
Yin and yang 13, 59; calligraphy and 104–106; demons and 73; funerals and 91; harmony and 61–63; in painting 101; relativity of 63
Yuan dynasty 51, 52; destruction of Taoist literature under 52

Zedong, Chairman Mao 112, 113
Zhang Dao Ling (Chang Tao Ling) 39–42, 67; as healer 41; immortality of 42
Zhang San Feng 11, 52–53
Zhang Zhue (Chang Chueh) 37, 39
Zhou (Chou) dynasty 18, 29, 30
Zhuangzi (Chuang Tzu) 25–29; explanation of Laozi by 26–27; explanation of Tao by 59
Zhuangzi 25–29; meditation and 92
Zhung Li (Chung-li) 18, 38, 69, 71